HEALING
LIFE'S
HURTS

Also by Ron Lee Davis:

Gold in the Making

A Forgiving God in an Unforgiving World

A Time for Compassion

Courage to Begin Again

HEALING LIFE'S HURTS

Discovering God's Grace in Discouragement, Conflict,
Mistreatment, Illness, Loss, Loneliness, Failure,
Inferiority, Doubt and Fear

Ron Lee Davis

with

James D. Denney

WORD PUBLISHING
Dallas · London · Sydney · Singapore

Library of Congress Cataloging-in-Publication Data

Davis, Ron Lee.
   Healing life's hurts.

   Bibliography: p.
   1. Christian life – 1960 –   . 2. Spiritual
healing. 3. Consolation. I. Title.
BV4501.2.D387   1968   248.8′ 6   86-1558
ISBN 0–8499–0466–8
ISBN 0-8499-3174-6 pbk.

Printed in the United States of America

9801239 BKC 987654321

To *Paul John Davis,*
my only brother, my best friend,
who taught me so much
about how to live,
and then about how to die;
who in life and in death
continually made
The Healing Choice.

Contents

HEALING LIFE'S HURTS

Prologue

Do You Want to Be Healed?

God permits us to go through deep waters, not to drown us, but to cleanse us.

—Anonymous

Now if we are children, then we are heirs—heirs of God and co-heirs with Christ, if indeed we share in his sufferings in order that we may also share in his glory.

—Romans 8:17

It was a Monday evening in July 1985, and I had just flown to Dallas for the Christian Booksellers Association Convention. The first draft of this book was nearly completed, and I was planning to discuss this material with my publisher and friend, Ernie Owen of Word Books. As I walked into the Hyatt-Regency Hotel where the Word Books reception was being held, my mind was focused two states away, consumed with thoughts and prayers for my brother Paul. For several weeks, he had been experiencing abdominal pains, and all the noninvasive medical tests had failed to yield a diagnosis. So now, at the same time I was in Dallas, my only brother and best friend was undergoing exploratory surgery in a Denver hospital.

I met Ernie Owen at the reception. We chatted briefly, agreeing to meet for breakfast the next morning to discuss details of the book. During the rest of the evening, I repeatedly left the reception and went to a pay phone in the lobby, placing call after call to the hospital in Denver. No one at the hospital could tell me anything about Paul's condition. I prayed and waited and continued calling until about 10:30 P.M., when a nurse finally told me Paul was out of surgery. She had orders, however, not to give out any other information over the phone.

More anxious than ever, I called Paul's home, hoping to speak with his wife, Jan. There was no answer. So next I called Marty Asbury, a good friend of Paul's. I knew Marty and his wife had stayed in the waiting room with my sister-in-law throughout Paul's surgery. "Jan just left a few minutes ago, but I can tell you what the doctors found," Marty told me. "Ron, Paul has cancer."

Cancer. The word penetrated like a knife. I tried to speak, but I couldn't. Instead, I found I was weeping. *I should have been there,* I thought. *I should have been with Jan and the boys when the doctors gave them the news.*

Marty went on, "It apparently began in the appendix, which is very rare, and it's spread to several other organs. The doctors think there's cancer in the liver, but they won't know for sure until the tests are in tomorrow. I'm sorry, Ron, but the doctors just aren't very optimistic. They only give Paul about six to twelve months."

My next call was to the airlines; I booked a 6 A.M. flight to Denver. The next morning, a few minutes before my departure, I called Ernie Owen from the airport and broke our breakfast appointment. Telling him I was going to Denver to be with my brother, I briefly explained the situation. Ernie graciously offered a prayer for our family over the phone and assured me that he and others at Word Books would be praying for Paul in the days ahead.

I landed in Denver and took a cab to the hospital, arriving just a few minutes before Jan. She and I were both with Paul when the doctor came in and explained to him that he had an advanced cancer. Paul took the news with amazing steadiness and replied that he was ready to fight it any way he could. He asked simply, "What do we do now?"

In the weeks that followed, I made several more trips between Denver and my home in California. During one of those trips to Denver, I stayed day and night in Paul's hospital room while he underwent chemotherapy immediately after his completion of five weeks of radiation treatments. During those difficult days and long nights, whenever the pain and nausea of the chemotherapy would subside, Paul and I had many opportunities to talk. We reminisced about growing up together in a small town in Iowa; and we talked of life and death and how Paul's faith in Christ was carrying him through this crisis.

He shared very openly with me his fears regarding the future and his concern for his wife and two teenage sons should this cancer take his life. We wept and prayed together many times, and I never felt closer to Paul than I did in those hours.

During those weeks, I watched Paul—who for over twenty years had been a coach to hundreds of young men, conducting basketball clinics around the country, active in the Fellowship of Christian Athletes—as he reached out from his hospital bed to touch the lives of young men whom he had already influenced powerfully for Christ. I saw tears streaming down the lean, tanned faces of rugged athletes as they dropped all their "macho" pretenses and wept openly at Paul's bedside.

It was only two months after Paul's cancer was first diagnosed that he suddenly began to develop serious complications. When we received the news, my mother flew to Denver from Iowa, and I again flew back from California. In his hospital room, my mother was able to tell Paul how much she loved him and what a wonderful son he'd been. I stayed through that night beside Paul's bed as he alternated between sleep and wakefulness. When he was awake, we talked, sharing thoughts and memories and prayers. During those long midnight hours in that darkened hospital room, Paul was as close to God as I had ever seen him.

At 8:00 the next morning, Jan and I hugged him and prayed with him as he was wheeled down the hallway to surgery. We stopped at the door that led to the operating room, and I kissed Paul on the neck and told him I loved him. He told me he loved me. Then he and Jan had a few precious moments together, and at last Paul was taken into surgery. That was the last conversation Jan and I had with Paul in this life. Despite the doctors' best efforts, the surgery was unable to extend Paul's life any further. The next morning, my brother—my closest friend—passed from this life into eternity.

The God of all mercy and comfort

As I write these words, it has only been a few weeks since Paul's death. There are a lot of things I still have to sort out, understand, and accept about Paul's suffering with cancer and his death at the age of forty-one. I know that time will never fully heal this sorrow I feel for the loss of my brother.

I know this is true because there are still many times when I feel the loss of my father as keenly as if it were yesterday, even though it has been twelve years since he died. Time *doesn't* heal all wounds. I expect the grief I feel for Paul to recur again and again as long as I live—and that's as it should be. When we love someone deeply, it hurts us deeply to let him or her go.

Still, despite the sorrow, the unanswered questions, and the trials and tears that continue in my life, I know peace. And while Paul's death is still too close and too painful for me to understand all the reasons for it, I believe I do have at least a faint and partial glimmer of one reason for some of the tragedy that comes into our lives. I'm convinced that our own grief and pain give us something authentic to share with others who are going through trials. By some process I don't fully understand, God is able to take the wounds and scars of our lives and transform them into a source of healing in the lives of others.

In 2 Corinthians, the apostle Paul tells us that God is

the source of all mercy and comfort. [And he] gives us comfort in all our trials so that we in turn may be able to give the same sort of strong sympathy to others in their troubles . . . Indeed, experience shows that the more we share in Christ's immeasurable suffering the more we are able to give of his encouragement. This means that if we experience trouble it is for your comfort and spiritual protection; for if we ourselves have been comforted we know how to encourage you to endure patiently the same sort of troubles that we have ourselves endured (1:3–6, PHILLIPS).

More than ever before, I'm coming to realize that God gives us His comfort in our trials to make us His ministers of healing to others in their trials. So I've felt a need in this book to be very open with you about my own hurts—not because I'm prepared as yet to make any profound applications from this experience, but to let you know as you are reading this book that I hurt along with you.

As I've talked with many people over the years about their problems and trials, I've found ten particular forms of trial to be the most difficult hurts of life: discouragement, conflict, mistreatment, illness, loss, loneliness, failure, inferiority, doubt, and fear. From time to time, I've personally wrestled with *each* of these areas in my own life. I struggle with some of these hurts even as I'm writing these words. So I hope you'll find in this book not only some encouragement and insight for your time of trial, but some consolation in the simple fact that these words are written by someone who can identify— at least to some limited degree—with your hurts.

In these days, I know what it means to hurt deeply over the death of a brother, of a close and irreplaceable friend. At the same time I've also been watching my mother, who has recently come to live with us, as she has been grieving over the death of a son. In all this I'm reminded of the fact that we have a God who also knows what it means to hurt over the death of a Son, Jesus Christ. God's love far exceeds any human love, and so if to love deeply means to hurt deeply in times of loss, then God who loves *perfectly* must have known the greatest pangs of loss and sorrow ever felt. This same Father, the God of all mercy and comfort, is alongside us in our trials, hurting along with us, mingling His tears with our own.

The pulse of pain

I suppose we could not find any more real pulse of mankind than the pulse of *pain*. The Word of God throbs with the pulsation of human pain. The words of David: "Many are the trials of the righteous." Job: "Man's days are short-lived and full of turmoil." Jesus: "In this world you shall have tribulation." Paul: "No one should be unsettled by these trials for you know quite well that we were destined for them." Peter: "Do not think it strange concerning the fiery trial which is to try you."

Trials are inescapable. In this life, we will encounter hurts and trials that we will not be able to change. We're just going to have to allow them to *change us.* In times of trial God has our undivided attention. We are aware of God and of our own limitations and powerlessness. But the question is: Are we teachable? Are we attentive to the way He wants to touch us, to the lesson He wants to show us? Trials call us to make a response to God.

There's a choice we have to make: We can decide to cooperate with God in our trial and seek His healing—if not a healing of the trial itself, then at least a healing of our attitude and emotions and character. *Or* we can choose bitterness, resentment, and self-pity.

Do you really want to be healed? When I'm counseling others or facing a rocky time in my own life, I am often reminded of the way Jesus penetrated one man's self-pity with this question. The story is found in John 5. Picture the scene with me:

A man lay by a large public pool. Helpless and paralyzed, he had been an invalid for thirty-eight years. He was one of scores of blind or crippled people gathered around this pool because of a local legend that an angel periodically came down, stirred the water, and imparted healing power to the pool. This man was waiting, passively and self-pityingly, without hope, without expectation.

A shadow fell across the paralyzed man where he lay. He looked up and saw that a man stood over him, piercing him with His gaze. "What do you want with me?" asked the paralyzed man.

The man eyed him levelly, "Do you want to be healed?"

At first glance, this might seem an astoundingly insensitive question. Who would be so cruel as to go up to an invalid and ask, "Do you want to be healed?" But in the original language of this Scripture passage, this is a much more penetrating question than that. What Jesus really asked this man was, "Do you *will* to be healed? Do you *choose* to be healed? Are you actively *committed* to the process of your own healing?" It was a question of the man's commitment to becoming whole.

This same question confronts you and me today. It's a question I raise all the time in my counseling with people who are struggling with deep depression, with self-pity, with a low sense of self-worth, with conflict in their marriage or other relationships: Are you actively *choosing* to have healing and maturity come forth in your life? Or do you just want my approval for your actions? Or do you just want someone to sympathize with all your woes?

I believe the reason Jesus asked this question of the paralyzed man was that He knew this man was filled with a blame mentality. When Jesus asked him, "Do you choose to be healed?" the man replied not with an answer but with an excuse: "No one will help me into the pool—and when I try to get in myself, someone else pushes ahead of me." But Jesus wasn't interested in this man's excuses.

The blame game is the oldest one in the world. In Genesis 3, immediately after the first sin in Eden, God confronted Adam with his sin. And Adam's reply was a masterpiece of blamesmanship: "The woman *you* put here with me—*she* gave me some fruit from the tree, and I ate it." In one finely tuned excuse, Adam managed to shift the blame two ways—onto Eve, who gave him the fruit, and onto God, who gave him Eve.

You may not have caused the trial you are experiencing. In fact, the circumstances of your trial may be completely unfair. But just as God wasn't interested in the excuses of Adam, just as Jesus wasn't interested in the excuses of the paralytic, neither is He interested in our excuses today. There was nothing fair or just about a man spending thirty-eight years of his life in paralysis and neglect—yet Jesus didn't ask him, "How has life been treating you?" but rather "Do you want to be healed?"

God is asking you and me the same question today. And if our answer is "Yes, Lord, I *choose* to be healed according to your will," then the next words He speaks to us are like those Jesus spoke to the paralyzed man by the pool. "Get up!" He tells us. "Quit making excuses! Make a *decision* to become whole! Get up out of that trough of self-pity and *start walking!*"

The cost

Do you want to be healed? If your answer is a bold, honest, courageous *Yes,* then here is how you must begin: Don't blame others anymore. Don't blame circumstances. Don't blame God. Get rid of your excuses. Commit yourself to doing whatever is necessary in partnership with God to find His chosen form of healing in your life. *Shoulder your responsibility for becoming whole.*

You may say, "I can't do that. It's going to hurt too much." Yes, there's *pain* involved in the process of gaining growth and wholeness. That's why so many of us shrink from that process. We would rather live with our brokenness, our neurosis, our emotional, spiritual, or relational disease than to *deal* with it decisively and courageously. We endure the throbbing ache of our disease because we fear the sharp, surgical touch of the Great Physician's healing scalpel. And so we *choose* to be tragically less than God wants us to be!

So this is *The Healing Choice* for all the hurts and trials of life: "Do you *truly* want to be healed?" To say "Yes" to this question will mean pain—the pain of honest self-appraisal and confession, the pain of taking responsibility for our own lives. To say, "Yes, I *choose* to be healed," is going to be costly.

But to say "No" will cost us even more.

1

Healing the Hurt
of Discouragement

There can be no rainbow without a cloud and a storm.

—J. H. Vincent

We are pressed on every side by troubles, but not crushed and broken. We are perplexed because we don't know why things happen as they do, but we don't give up and quit. We are hunted down, but God never abandons us. We get knocked down, but we get up again and keep going.

—2 Corinthians 4:8–9 (LB)

My friend John Huffman, the pastor of St. Andrew's Presbyterian Church in Newport Beach, California, recently shared a story with me that was told him by his long-time friend, Bertha Spafford Vester. Mrs. Vester, who passed away a number of years ago, was the daughter of a wealthy Chicago businessman named Horatio Spafford, and the story she told my friend John was one that took place in her family before she was born.

In late 1873, Horatio Spafford saw his wife, Anna, and their four children aboard the ocean liner *Ville du Havre*, bound from New York to France. Spafford had some business affairs to conclude in the States before he could rejoin his family in Europe. The journey of the *Ville du Havre* proceeded smoothly until sometime after midnight on November 22, when the vessel was rammed broadside by another vessel, the *Lochearn*.

As the wounded *Ville du Havre* settled heavily into the midnight sea, violently rushing waters separated Mrs. Spafford from the three oldest children. She still clutched her youngest child, little Tannetta, as the swirling water swept her into the cold Atlantic. Suddenly, the child was torn from her grasp. Mrs. Spafford frantically sought her only remaining child in

23

the darkness, caught the hem of her gown for a moment, then lost it. She fell unconscious and was later pulled from the water by sailors from the *Lochearn.* Her four children were drowned.

A few days later, Horatio Spafford received a telegram stating that his wife had been saved from the sinking of the *Ville du Havre,* but all four of his children had been lost at sea. Spafford fell into an unrelievable gloom. In New York, he boarded a ship for Europe to join his wife. At a certain point in the voyage, the captain of the ship announced that they were passing the site of the wreck of the *Ville du Havre.* Spafford stood at the rail and peered into the depths of the sea that had shipwrecked his family and swallowed his four children. Then he returned to his cabin and began composing the opening lines of one of the most moving hymns ever written:

> When peace, like a river, attendeth my way,
> When sorrows like sea billows roll,
> Whatever my lot, Thou has taught me to say,
> It is well, it is well with my soul.

Spafford well knew the meaning of the words "sorrows like sea billows." Yet burdened as he was with depression and grief, he was able to find a kind of inner peace. He was learning to say, even in the depths of his discouragement, "It is well with my soul."

Shipwrecked!

The hurt of discouragement takes varied forms in different lives: The estrangement of friends, parents, or children. The ruin of one's reputation. Financial failure. A failed marriage or a love relationship that has grown cold. Inability to build good habits or to break bad ones. Stress at work or in the home.

Whatever form your trial of discouragement takes, it almost always involves a sense that life has let you down. It's the feeling described in the motion picture *The Natural* when the story's aging baseball player, Roy Hobbs (played by Robert Redford), looks back on his life and grimly observes, "Life hasn't turned out the way I thought it would." It hurts to go on, and you feel defeated and worn down. You had set out in one direction, but the storms of life have arisen and tossed you the other way. Now you feel you've been beached on an obscure island, far from the course you charted for yourself.

The apostle Paul knew that feeling. The closing chapters of the Book of Acts tell us that Paul was determined to take the gospel of Jesus Christ to the very pinnacle of the Roman empire, the city of Rome—even if it meant going as a prisoner in chains. Confined in Roman custody, Paul was placed on a ship with other prisoners, bound for Rome. But along the way, hurricane winds rose up, driving their ship relentlessly across the angry Mediterranean. After two weeks of being tossed about by the storm, most of those on board despaired of ever being saved. Finally the ship ran aground and broke apart, spilling Paul and his 275 shipmates onto a cold and windy beach on the island of Malta.

As I've considered this story, I've wondered what was going through Paul's mind as he pulled himself out of the surf and dropped in exhaustion onto the beach. His plans, his timetable had been dashed to pieces. Now he was drenched, cold, hungry—and he had a choice to make: he could either yield to the discouragement and defeat of this catastrophe, or he could make the healing choice, the choice to become God's man for the crisis.

Acts 27 records the decision Paul made. He saw that there was a vacuum of leadership, so he *emerged* in leadership. He gave encouragement to his 275 discouraged fellow-castaways. He told them to take courage because God was with them. He urged them to take nourishment, and then he gave thanks to God, broke bread, and ate it. His shipmates began to follow his lead, drawing encouragement from his example. In the midst of discouraging circumstances, Paul refused to be defeated. Rather, he made the choice to be an encourager to the discouraged, an example to those in despair.

Paul knew how it felt to be shipwrecked, and perhaps you know the feeling too. In your career, your ministry, your family, or your schoolwork, you have certain goals. And for a long time you believed God was drawing you toward those goals. But you've fallen into discouraging circumstances. You feel as though God has led you to a dead end. You're confused about His will and discouraged about your life. You feel shipwrecked.

I've known that feeling myself. In my own life and in the lives of others, I've noticed a tendency which I believe may be at the root of much of our discouragement: We sense that God is calling us to some new adventure, and then *we* decide how we're going to get there, how long it's going to take, and what route we're going to travel. But somewhere along the way, it dawns on us that God's timetable doesn't coincide with ours. His schedule for us includes some layovers, some setbacks, some storms, some things we never anticipated. The inevitable result is discouragement, and we even begin to doubt God's plan and His love for us.

But God *does* love us and He *does* have a plan for our lives. Why, then, does His plan often permit us to undergo trials of discouragement? I believe one of the principal reasons God allows us to be tried is that He wants us to learn to have *His perspective* on both the good times and hard times of our lives. As C. S. Lewis once wrote, "It is a fact of Christian experience that life is a series of troughs and peaks. In His effort to get permanent possession of a soul, God relies on the troughs more than the peaks. And some of His special favorites have gone through longer and deeper troughs than anyone else." This is the same truth expressed by David in Psalm 119:71—"It was good for me to be afflicted so that I might learn your decrees." We learn about God and His truth through the discouraging times of our lives.

Now, you may feel you don't even *want* God's perspective. All you really want is for your discouraging circumstances to go away. That's understandable; when we've been deeply hurt, we all want an anesthetic much more than we want a lengthy process of healing. Yet we have to acknowledge that when we find ourselves powerless to alter our circumstances, we're going to have to alter our *response* to those circumstances—and that means we're going to have to find God's perspective for our discouragement.

In my own trials of discouragement I often recall the words of F. B. Meyer: "If I'm told I am to take a hard and dangerous journey, every jolt along the way will remind me I'm on the right path." Trials, perils, setbacks, and delays may discourage us—but viewed correctly, from God's perspective, these discouraging circumstances are actually the very reminders that we are on the *right* path, the hard path of following Jesus. That's the Christian life. It's your life, it's my life, and it was Paul's life too.

Paul looked discouragement squarely in the face—and then he made a choice to be God's man for the crisis. That's a choice we can all make, no matter what our circumstances may be. We can always make the healing choice to be God's person in a crisis of discouragement. Like Paul, we can acknowledge that God is with us, even in our deep discouragement, and He is still working out His plan in our lives. That's the bottom-line promise that runs throughout all of Scripture: God is with us. Psalm 23:4—"I will fear no evil, for you are with me." Jeremiah 1:8—"Do not be afraid . . . for I am with you." Matthew 28:20—"Surely I will be with you always, to the very end of the age."

Whatever our circumstances, God is with us. God was with John Gunther in the suffering and death of his little son, Johnny. In his book *Death Be Not Proud,* Gunther writes,

> During Johnny's long illness I prayed continually to God. Naturally, God was always there. He sat beside us during the doctor's consultation, as we waited the long vigils outside the operating room, as we rejoiced in the miracle of a brief recovery, as we agonized when hope ebbed away and the doctors confessed there was no longer anything they could do. They were helpless and we were helpless. But God in His infinite wisdom and mercy was standing by us.[1]

That's what the presence of God is like amid our sorrows, our disappointments, our discouragements: He cries with us and He hurts with us. In the presence of the God of all comfort there is encouragement for all our discouraging circumstances. And we can then take that encouragement and pass it on to others in the same way—by offering our presence to those who hurt, crying with them, hurting with them, being with them just as God is with us.

The apostle Paul once wrote that God comforts and encourages us so that we are enabled to "comfort those in any trouble with the comfort we ourselves have received from God" (2

Cor. 1:4). But do any of us ever really feel *adequate* to comfort someone else during their trial of grief or discouragement? We think, *I don't know what to do! I don't know what to say!* So all too often our response to someone else who is going through a period of discouragement is to do nothing and to say nothing.

Yet there's a very simple and effective ministry of comforting others that *everyone* can practice—a ministry of *simple presence* coupled with *practical encouragement.* You don't have to be able to deliver a comforting sermon or quote passages of Scripture. In fact, usually the most helpful thing you can do for a down-and-out friend is to simply say, "I want to spend some time with you. Would you like to go out for lunch?" It sounds too easy, but it's absolutely true: the most comforting thing you can do for a discouraged person is to offer your presence and some practical, everyday encouragement—encouragement such as:

"Have you been getting any sleep? Why don't you just go home early tonight and get eight solid hours of sleep?"

Or, "Could we just take your kids tonight? We know you've been going through a lot lately. Why don't you and your spouse go see a movie or just spend the evening alone together?"

Or, "You know, I'm a pretty good listener. I'd be glad to just stop by if you need somebody to talk to."

That's called *practical encouragement.* That's the kind of encouragement Paul gave to his discouraged shipmates after they had been storm-tossed for two weeks. "For the last fourteen days, you have been in constant suspense and have gone without food," he says in Acts 27:33–34. "I urge you to take some food. You need it to survive." Then he set an example, giving thanks for the little bread they had, breaking it, and eating it with them. A few hours later, their ship ran aground, and all hands were saved, perhaps in part because they had been strengthened by the practical encouragement of the apostle Paul.

Marie Rothenberg, in her book *David,* describes the ordeal of her six-year-old son David, whose father intentionally left him in a burning motel room in southern California in 1983.[2] Though he received third-degree burns over 90 percent of his body, David survived.

During the first few days of David's hospitalization, while

Marie was facing the agony and discouragement of watching her little boy suffer and struggle to live, she was approached by a Christian couple, Ken and Judy Curtis. Ken himself had discovered the presence and comfort of God during his recovery from an industrial accident in which he had been severely burned. Now he and his wife offered that same presence and practical encouragement to Marie, inviting her to stay in their home so she could be near the hospital where David was being treated.

Late one night, Marie returned to the Curtis home, angry and crying. Ken and Judy met her in the kitchen. "What happened?" they asked her. "Is Davie okay?"

"His ear fell off," Marie answered, "and I had to be the one who discovered it."

How did Ken and Judy Curtis respond? Ken offered her a chair: *practical encouragement.* Judy poured her a cup of tea: *practical encouragement.* Ken took her hand, offering no words, just a touch: *practical encouragement.* Judy prayed for her, simply and briefly: *practical encouragement.* And in her book Marie describes her response to the presence and practical encouragement of her friends, Ken and Judy: "As Judy prayed, I felt relieved . . . and I was grateful for Ken and Judy, who waited through the night to comfort me." [3]

When someone you know is feeling defeated, discouraged, depressed, and you don't have any words of comfort to offer, there is still something you can do to bring comfort and encouragement. You don't have to quote Scripture. You don't have to explain why God allows trials in our lives. All you need to do, and perhaps all you *can* do, is simply to offer down-to-earth, practical encouragement—a word of support, a touch, a brief prayer, a cup of tea, simple presence.

Why am I shipwrecked?

Anyone who has ever had to endure trials of deep discouragement would probably like to ask God some questions, such as, "Why does it seem there is so much trouble in the Christian life? Why do committed Christians so often find themselves disheartened, discouraged, and shipwrecked?" Let me suggest a few possible answers—partial answers, even just *glimpses* into the answers—which may help you come to a place of inner peace about your discouraging circumstances.

First of all, I'm convinced that one of the principal reasons we encounter trials of discouragement is because of the influence of Satan in this fallen world. The apostle Paul recorded several occasions in which he experienced the active opposition of Satan to his plans and dreams. For example, in 1 Thessalonians 2:18 he writes, "we wanted to come to you . . . but Satan stopped us." Paul was a man who knew the power of the resurrected Christ to change lives, and Satan continually sought to neutralize his effectiveness.

How should we respond to satanic attempts to discourage and deter us? The apostle John gives us the key: ". . . the one who is in you is greater than the one who is in the world" (1 John 4:4). God in us is greater than the evil god of this world. We will face hindrances and opposition, yet we can and will overcome all these evils because God is in us and with us. He is greater than our trials, greater than our discouragement—and the knowledge of His presence strengthens us to stand firm in the faith.

A second possible reason God allows trials of discouragement in our lives is He wants us to be involved in the lives of others. Whether we are aware of it or not, we continually influence those around us, either for good or ill—and it's in the storms of life that our influence on others is distilled and concentrated. People look to our example and watch how we respond under pressure. The choices we make when we are hurting and discouraged—including our choice of *attitude*— will have a profound impact on friends and loved ones, fellow Christians and non-Christians, and most of all on our families.

Paul made the healing choice to be a positive, encouraging influence on those who were shipwrecked with him. He took his crisis and turned it into an opportunity for witness and ministry to others. Instead of cursing his bad luck, he led, he prayed, and he exhorted. In his trial of discouragement, Paul made the choice to offer himself as God's channel of blessing and healing to others. You and I can make this same choice as we face our discouraging circumstances.

After her husband and four other missionaries were murdered by Auca Indians in Ecuador, Elisabeth Elliot made a decision to bring good out of a seemingly senseless tragedy. Courageously she chose to offer her trial of grief and discouragement to God so that He could transform it into ministry to others. After many weeks in prayer, she sensed that God was leading her to go to the Aucas who had killed her husband, Jim Elliot, and carry on his work among them.

Months later, Elisabeth Elliot stood in the Auca village which had been her husband's objective, sharing the gospel with the same men who had murdered the five missionaries. Touched by her forgiveness and love, these men gave their hearts to Jesus Christ and were later baptized in the river where the slaughter had taken place. Next, the Aucas themselves baptized the children of Jim Elliot and the other slain missionaries. That day, the waters that had once flowed with the blood of martyrs became a river of healing and forgiveness.

But the story doesn't end there. The Auca Christians were so transformed by the forgiveness and love that had been modeled toward them that they decided to go to an enemy tribe downstream and tell them of the love of Jesus. They set off into danger—armed only with the gospel of peace.

The Aucas arrived at the encampment of the other tribe and were met by fierce warriors armed with arrows and spears. The Auca Christians offered no resistance, only love and forgiveness. One of them, named Tona, stood in his boat saying over and over to his enemies, "I forgive you! I forgive you! I am dying for your benefit!" Those were his last words before he was slain.

But even this is not the end of the story. This fierce downriver tribe, like the Aucas before them, ultimately yielded to the forgiving love of Christ. On and on, the gospel spread through this remote region of Ecuador, just as the gospel has spread throughout Christian history. God uses people like you and me, even in our most painful and discouraging circumstances, to influence others and work out His plan. We are to demonstrate to a watching world what Christian men and women are really like away from the safety of the harbor.

Another possible reason God allows trials of discouragement in our lives is that He wants to make us more mature, more like Christ. As Paul tells us in Romans 8:28–29, God works "in all things"—even our trials and discouraging circumstances—so that we might "be conformed to the likeness of his Son." He is building Christlike maturity into our character.

You may wonder, "Will I ever get to a place in life where

it's all smooth sailing, and God won't have to allow these trials in my life anymore?" Probably not. Trials and discouragements will always be with us. Look at Paul: Though he was approaching the end of his life and was full of faith, courage, and character, God allowed him to be shipwrecked. Why? Because Paul still had some lessons to learn about Christian maturity. So do we.

Daniel Poling, the former editor of *The Christian Herald,* had only one son. During World War II, Poling and his wife committed their son to God's care when he went to the South Pacific as a chaplain. The Polings and their son had a strong bond between them, and they exchanged letters often. In one of her letters to her son, Mrs. Poling wrote, "Son, I pray every day for your safety."

One day the Polings received a letter from their son which read in part, "Mom, don't just pray for my safety. Pray for my maturity." And that was the last letter the Polings received from him before he was killed in action.

What do we pray for in our own prayer life? Yes, we pray for safety—but do we also pray for maturity? Do we only pray for a painless life—or do we pray even more for a *productive* life? God's goal for our lives is *Christlikeness*—conformity to the character of Jesus Christ—and He often uses stormy trials and shipwrecks to achieve His plan in us.

We know that God's strength is often perfected in our lives when we are at our weakest. In 2 Corinthians 12, Paul tells how he prayed repeatedly that God would remove from him a troubling physical affliction, a "thorn in the flesh." God answered Paul's prayers, "My grace is sufficient for you, for my power is made perfect in weakness." Many of us would be discouraged and tempted to give up in the face of a "No" answer to our prayers—but Paul made the healing choice to respond, "I delight in weaknesses, in insults, in hardships, in persecutions, in difficulties. For when I am weak, then I am strong."

Ultimately, as we are trying to understand why God allows trials of discouragement in our lives, we have to acknowledge that we will never fully know all the reasons. That's hard for many of us to accept. We feel that God should have given us those answers in the Bible, but what the Bible tells us is that "the secret things belong to the Lord our God" (Deut.

29:29). God is greater than our understanding, and in Him there are deep mysteries we are unable to penetrate in our lifetime.

During the time he was going through treatments for Hodgkin's disease, my friend Gid Adkisson told me, "I don't know what lessons I've learned from this, but I know God is with me and He is sovereign." Though lacking all the answers for his discouraging circumstances, Gid was still able to trust in God. He experienced the presence of God and received practical encouragement from many of his Christian friends—but there were mysteries and questions that would have to go unanswered, and he accepted that by faith. He was living by the truth of 1 Corinthians 13:12—"Now we see but a poor reflection; then we shall see face to face. Now I know in part; then I shall know fully, even as I am fully known."

Someone believes in you

Some time ago, my friend Bruce Larson was vacationing in the Bahamas. One day as he was walking along the beach, he saw a crowd gathered on a pier. He went closer to investigate and found the focus of attention to be a young man preparing for a solo around-the-world journey in a homemade sailboat. All of those who crowded around the pier were trying to discourage the ambitious young sailor:

"The sun will broil the skin right off of you!"

"You'll run out of drinking water!"

"That little boat will never make it!"

The boat pushed away from the pier and began moving out across the blue Caribbean waters, followed by jeers and ridicule from the shore. Bruce was suddenly seized by an irresistible impulse to offer some encouragement to the young man, so he began running along the pier, waving his arms and shouting, "Bon voyage! We're with you! We believe in you! You can do it!" The young man smiled and waved back at Bruce, then continued on until he was out of sight over the horizon.

Like that young man in his frail boat, we're on a journey through life. There may be storms and delays ahead. There may even be a shipwreck in our future. Sometimes we feel there are more people waiting for us to fail than there are people cheering us on. We need to know someone is pulling for us, believing in us. The young voyager in the tiny sailboat had only one supporter the day he set sail—but he eventually made it completely around the globe.

Where are you on your voyage today?

Even though you may feel as though you're ditched on an obscure beach, God has promised to be with you. He's piloting you to a safe and secure harbor. Whatever your storm or shipwreck right now, God is pulling for you, cheering you on, and He wants to give you His healing for your hurt, His strength for your weakness, and His courage for your discouragement.

2

Healing the Hurt of Illness

Healing in Scripture does not refer to becoming as you were; it is becoming what you should be.
—Charles Farr

Heal me, O Lord, and I will be healed; save me and I will be saved, for you are the one I praise.
—Jeremiah 17:14

When Richard, a close friend of mine, was diagnosed as having a terminal illness, he and his family began to pray to God for healing. According to the medical literature, the diagnosis was practically a death sentence. As his condition began to worsen, Richard and his family began to seek out the help of several of the most famous faith healers in the country. Many of them promised without qualification, "Jesus wants you to be healed"—in effect, an unconditional guarantee that Richard would be delivered from his disease.

It was just a short time ago that Richard died at the age of thirty-two. Until just a few days before his death, Richard and his family were certain that God was going to physically heal him. But God *didn't* heal him—at least not in the way they sought. Richard's faith ran deep, and he made the hard adjustment from believing God was going to deliver him from his illness to the painful truth: the only way out of this illness was through the door of Death itself.

Shortly before Richard's memorial service, I was talking and praying with his father and his young widow. When the subject of the inscription on Richard's headstone came up, his father suggested a few lines from Scripture. "No!" Richard's grieving wife interrupted, "How can we put a Scripture verse on Richard's headstone? If we can't believe what the Bible says about healing, then how can we believe any of it?"

If you had been me, how would you have responded? Prominent faith healers had given Richard and his wife false assurances about healing, and the shattering of those illusions shook her faith and deepened her grief. Miraculously, her faith survived. She has accepted God's will for Richard, and says that his being at home with the Lord is "the ultimate healing." She continues to work through her questions toward deeper trust in God. But how many people have actually had their faith completely broken by a misunderstanding of God's healing for the hurt of illness?

A few years ago, Carol, a young woman in the Midwest, became a Christian following an accident which left her a paraplegic. From her wheelchair she wrote:

> Someone told me just after I became a Christian that God would heal me. This seemed too good to be true. I didn't know if I dared believe it. But I began to hope, and then to believe. Day after day, I prayed to be healed, but I remained a paraplegic.
>
> I began to realize that God had the power to heal me, but that He wasn't going to heal me. I became increasingly bitter. I would read about healing in the Bible, then accuse God of holding the promise of healing before me like a piece of meat before a starving dog. He taunted me by showing me the potential, but never quite allowing me to reach it. Then I would feel guilty because I know the Bible says God is a loving God and answerable to no one.
>
> My conflict deepened, and my mental state became precarious. I've considered suicide many times. Over and over I have asked God why He refuses to heal me, but I get no reply.

How would you respond to the plea of this physically and spiritually wounded young woman?

Blaming the victim

Many of us feel very confused about the hurt of illness. Where is God when sickness enters our lives or the life of

someone close to us? Do miracles of healing still happen—
or are they just something we read about in the Bible? In
an article in *Christianity Today,* surgeon Paul Brand frankly
assesses the failure of the church to deal realistically and forth-
rightly with these questions:

> God neither protects Christians with a shield of health
> nor provides a quick, dependable solution to all suffering.
> Christians populate hospital wards, asylums, and cancer
> hospices in approximate proportion to the world at large.
> Many Christians who roll in wheelchairs, or awake each
> day to the scarred stumps of amputated limbs, or undergo
> the debility of spreading cancer have prayed for healing.
> Some have attended healing services, felt a sudden rush
> of hope, and kneeled for an anointing of oil; yet still they
> live unhealed. For them, divine healing is the cruelest
> joke of all. At the precise moment when they most need
> support from the church they receive instead a taunting
> accusation that in spiritual as well as physical health they
> do not measure up.[1]

It is one of the most common tragedies in the church today:
a Christian who is already struggling with the hurt of illness
has his suffering compounded by accusation and guilt. "It's
never God's will for Christians to suffer," say some advocates
of divine healing, "so your suffering must either be due to
unconfessed sin in your life or lack of faith to let God heal
you." In effect, the victim is *blamed* for his disease.

In an article she wrote, Kathryn Lindskoog describes the
remarks she has endured during two decades of suffering with
multiple sclerosis (MS), a chronic disease that gradually weak-
ens and paralyzes the body. A few typical examples:

> "You must really like to be sick; you bring so much
> of it on yourself." That from a nearby relative who never
> so much as sent a get-well card.
> "The reason I have perfect health is that I think right;
> nobody gets sick unless he thinks wrong." That from a
> relative who seems to feel insecure about all his good
> luck in life. . . .
> "Dear, if your faith is sincere, tell everyone right now
> that God has healed you completely." That from a friend
> who couldn't wait to report such a claim to her Bible
> study.

"I know just how you feel about being crippled; I had a bad case of tennis elbow last month." That from one of the local country club crowd. . . .

"God must cherish you to trust you with this burden." That from people who would rather die than to be cherished by such a God.

"Your present improvement is just wishful thinking." That from people who are very rigid about sticking to current medical orthodoxy.

"I know you fake your limp to try to get attention." An entirely serious remark from my pastor after a dozen years of seeing me hobble around our large church complex. That's the one I haven't gotten over yet.[2]

These statements reported by Kathryn Lindskoog may seem bizarre, but I would affirm that they are not at all unusual. While my brother Paul was being treated for cancer and following his death, I received many comments from people who clearly meant well, but who were simply no comfort in that time of trial. In particular there were two things people said to me that I found were not at all helpful: "Time heals all wounds," and "God will use greatly only those He has hurt deeply."

Some people feel awkward in the presence of a suffering person and simply feel a need to fill up the silence. Others genuinely want to offer comfort but don't really know what to say. My own experience is that often the greatest comfort is offered in the fewest words. Simple presence, a touch, an embrace, a brief prayer: these can be the greatest comfort of all in a trial of illness.

The miracle of prayer

Our deep need in times of illness is to grasp firmly what His healing really means in our lives. We approach the Great Physician as unique individuals, and His prescription for your health and mine will vary according to our individual need. We may need emotional and spiritual healing even more than we need bodily health. But what if He chooses to heal us physically? Does that mean we should be looking for a miracle?

Unfortunately, in our fascination with the miraculous and the sensational, we often fail to recognize the everyday miracles

God engineers throughout our lives. Properly viewed, *every* recovery from illness or injury is a kind of divine miracle. The human body has been marvelously engineered to protect and repair itself. It contains elaborate, intricate systems for fighting off infection, repairing lacerated tissue, mending broken bones, and repairing diseased organ tissue—and the actual mechanism by which these systems keep us healthy is either incompletely known or totally hidden to medical science.

In an episode of the television series *M*A*S*H*, Army surgeon Hawkeye Pierce (portrayed by Alan Alda) expressed amazement over the self-perpetuating, self-repairing human body. "How does it all work?" he wondered. "I've held a beating heart in my hand. I've poked into kidneys and crocheted them together again. I've pushed air into collapsed lungs like beat-up old pump organs. I've squeezed and probed and prodded my way through hundreds of miles of gut and goo, and I don't know what makes us live! I mean, what keeps us in motion? What keeps the heart beating without anybody rewinding it? Why do the cells reproduce and then re-re-re-produce with such gay abandon? What force brought us together in such fantastic complexity? I've seen a lot of bodies, and it never ceases to amaze me." Or as the Psalmist more succinctly put it, we are "fearfully and wonderfully made."

In *The Road Less Traveled,* Dr. M. Scott Peck observes that the so-called "normal" biological systems that keep us alive and give us our resistance to disease and injury are, in fact, completely *miraculous.* He writes:

> In the ordinary course of things we should be eaten alive by bacteria, consumed by cancer, clogged up by fats and clots, eroded by acids. It is hardly remarkable that we sicken and die; what is truly remarkable is that we don't usually sicken very often and we don't die very quickly. . . . There is a force, the mechanism of which we do not fully understand, that seems to operate routinely in most people to protect and encourage their physical health even under the most adverse conditions.[3]

This dimly understood "force," Peck suggests, is actually God's sustaining *grace* in our lives. God's grace to us, which we so often take for granted, is nothing short of miraculous—or, as one hymnwriter termed it, *amazing;* " 'Tis *grace* hath brought me safe thus far," he wrote—and it's true: God's amazing grace protects us, nurtures us, and heals us in ways that we tend to overlook. Healing, then, is not usually an *event;* rather, it is most often a process. The process of healing takes time—but it is through our time of healing that we gain a greater sense of God's grace and His presence with us.

There is another miraculous dimension to the healing process: the miracle of *prayer.* God gives us immediate access to Himself any time, any place, for any reason. We can call upon the sovereign God of the Universe, and know He has the power to heal—and that gives us hope. That is why Hebrews 4:16 tells us, "Let us then approach the throne of grace with confidence, so that we may receive mercy and find grace to help us in our time of need."

How, then, should we pray for healing?

First, we have to acknowledge that there is no formula, no ritual, no magic word to coax God into healing us according to our will. The sovereignty of God calls us to humility: if He is truly Lord, then it is *His* will that must be done, not our own. Yes, we raise our honest petitions before Him in prayer, and we ask Him to heal—and then we listen for His answer: *Yes.* Or, *No.* Or, *Wait.*

We know that when we pray for healing, we must pray in faith. But we wonder, "How much is *enough* faith?" In Matthew 17:20, Jesus says all we need is "faith as small as a mustard seed." The tiniest particle of faith is sufficient. A distraught father once brought his son to Jesus for healing, and his prayer to Jesus was, "Take pity on us and help us!" Jesus told him that all things are possible to those who believe. At that the father cried, "I *do* believe! Help me overcome my unbelief!" That is a mustard seed prayer, and God has promised to honor that prayer.

Sickness is hard on faith. A crisis of pain can quickly become a trial of doubt. Job was an upright man who walked closely with God, yet his trial of illness pressed his faith right to the wall. This is only natural. If illness is causing you to doubt and cry out to God, don't feel as though you've lost your faith. The mustard seed of your faith is still there, even though hemmed in by pain. God is still at work in your life, answering your prayers.

The Bible gives us a pattern for prayer when we find ourselves in a trial of illness. This is not a formula for manipulating God, but a means of prayerfully preparing *ourselves*—body, mind, and soul—to receive God's healing touch in our lives. God doesn't want to merely remove our symptoms, but to *heal* us in a thorough, integrated way. He doesn't just want to make us feel better; He wants to make us *whole.* So as I've studied the Scriptures, I've found this biblical pattern for prayer in times of illness:

1. *Worship.* This is the first and foremost aspect of *all* prayer. Worship is honest acknowledgment of God's holiness, power, and complete sovereignty. Worship is not just our duty toward God; it's our *joy!* As we worship God, we become aware of His authority over all things, including disease—and that gives us hope.

2. *Confess and be forgiven.* Prayer is hindered by sin in the life of the one who prays, so confession and forgiveness are always a vital part of effective prayer. Since God desires not just our physical wellness, but our *wholeness* in body, mind, and spirit, we find a close linkage of healing and forgiveness in the Bible. Thus James 5:15–16 (NASB) says, "The prayer offered in faith will restore the one who is sick, and the Lord will raise him up, and if he has committed sins, they will be forgiven him. Therefore, confess your sins to one another, and pray for one another, so that you may be healed."

3. *Listen for guidance and wisdom.* As we pray, we seek to think God's thoughts after Him, not tell Him what to do. It takes a lot of wisdom to discern God's answer to our prayers because His answers often differ from our expectations. James 1:5 tells us, "If any of you lacks wisdom, he should ask God, who gives generously to all without finding fault, and it will be given to him." Unless we continually seek God's wisdom for our trial of illness, we risk missing the answer he gives us.

4. *Petition.* We must ask God for healing. This seems obvious—yet we all too often treat prayer as the final act of desperation when all else has failed. The simple truth of James 4:2 is "You do not have, because you do not ask God." In times of trial, prayer should be our first impulse, not our last resort. Listen to the prayer of David in Psalm 6:2–3, "Be merciful to me, Lord, for I am faint! O Lord, heal me, for my bones

are in agony! My soul is in anguish! How long, O Lord, how long?" A time of illness calls us to lay our honest feelings, our pain, and our plea for healing before the throne of God's healing grace.

5. *Request the prayers and anointing of the elders.* "Is any one of you sick?" says James 5:14. "He should call the elders of the church to pray over him and anoint him with oil in the name of the Lord." One way we can demonstrate our desire to make the healing choice for our illness is to take the initiative to call the elders to come and pray for our healing.

Notice, too, that the oil mentioned in James 5:14 was the common, accepted medical treatment for most ills in the first century—not a magical potion. In this passage God calls us to cooperate with the best medical expertise available in order to bring about our healing; the oil is merely a *symbol* of our commitment to seek God's chosen form of healing.

6. *Request the prayers and encouragement of others.* The pain of illness can often cloud our ability to pray effectively to God. But we're not alone in our illness. God has given us Christian brothers and sisters to love us, encourage us, and uphold us with their prayers. As Rev. Charles Farr, pastor of the Church of the Epiphany in Denver, said,

> We often mistakenly assume that faith has to come from the sick. The faith of anyone who is suffering is likely to be diminished. We would never expect a child who is sick to get up, prepare his own food, and nourish himself. Why do we expect hurting people to heal themselves with exemplary faith?
> Remember the story of the paralytic in Scripture? . . . The man's friends took him to the housetop, removed the tiles around the hole where the cooking fire was vented, and with ropes they lowered the man on his pallet into Jesus' presence. Jesus, seeing *"their* faith," not the man's faith, told him to take up his bed and walk.[4]

James 5:16 tells us, "Pray for each other so that you may be healed." It was never intended we suffer our illness alone. We need each other in the body of Christ.

7. *Wait upon God.* When you have prayed, when others have prayed for you, when everything medically possible has been done, then *wait.* Allow God to work. Give Him time

to answer. And be open to His answer—whatever it is. Paul
Tillich once wrote that prayer gives us access to "a power
that shakes us and turns us, and transforms us and heals us.
Surrender to this power is faith." So as we pray for healing,
we need to surrender to God, by faith allowing Him to heal
as He chooses.

The ultimate form of healing

I believe God always heals—but we have to be open to
whatever *form* of healing God chooses to bring into our lives.
He may touch us through a sudden miracle or through a
lengthy healing process or by giving us His sufficient grace
to endure a trial of illness that won't go away.

The ultimate form of healing that every believer faces one
day is physical death and bodily resurrection. Paul, in Romans
8:18 and 23, shares his strong assurance, "I consider that our
present sufferings are not worth comparing with the glory that
will be revealed in us. . . . We ourselves, who have the first-
fruits of the Spirit, groan inwardly as we wait eagerly for . . .
the redemption of our bodies."

Charles Farr put it this way: "God wants us to be healed
even if that means dying well. Health is being at peace with
God and at peace with yourself." This is a *biblical* definition
of health; it agrees with the witness of Scripture: "Heal me,
O Lord, and I will be healed; save me and I will be saved,
for you are the one I praise" (Jer. 17:14). And Isaiah 53:5
tells us that Christ suffered and died to purchase our *peace*—
peace with God, peace with ourselves—"and by his wounds
we are healed." Healed—even in our trials, even in our pain,
even in death itself. We can live well and die well, at peace
with God, filled with the healing assurance of eternal life.

Can we believe in miracles of healing? I believe the answer
to that question is an emphatic *Yes!* I've seen God dramatically
heal. My friend Ruth, a woman in her early fifties, was conclu-
sively diagnosed as having an advanced form of cancer that
is usually fatal. So Ruth did what any of us would do: she
prayed and asked God to give her a miracle of healing.

She followed the admonition of James 5: She first made
sure to follow her doctors' advice and was scheduled to begin
treatments almost immediately. Then she called me and asked

that I call some of the elders of our church to her bedside to pray for her and anoint her. We went to her home that evening, and as I was about to lead in prayer Ruth said, "Ron, I want to be healed, and I know God *can* heal me. But what I really want you to pray for is that God will heal me the way He thinks best. Pray that I have the strength to learn whatever He wants to teach me through this trial."

We honored her wish and prayed for her in the way she asked us to. We anointed her with oil as a symbol of her commitment to seek God's form of healing. A short time later, when Ruth went to the hospital for treatment and tests, the doctors were astonished to find that her cancer had completely disappeared. That was almost ten years ago, and Ruth is alive and well today. But the most important thing about Ruth's story is the demonstration of her faith in God: she humbly submitted herself to God's will for her life—even if the way to freedom from cancer led right through the Grave itself.

David Ireland, in his book *Letters to an Unborn Child,* described the attitude with which he faced his incurable neurological disease:

> I have often asked myself, and have on occasion been asked by others, "Do I believe in faith healing?" I have never taken the matter lightly. On one occasion I asked a former bishop of the Methodist Church to lay his hands on me. Later I attended the service of a nationally known faith healer, not as an observer, but as one open to whatever God might will. In neither case did my failure to undergo a miracle in any way affect me negatively.
>
> Today when I'm asked, "Do you believe God will heal you?" my response is a question, one I have asked myself. "Do I really need to be healed?" It's a genuine question, not a mere defense to avoid the issue. . . . My faith is in the genuineness of God, not in whether He will do this or that to demonstrate His goodness. I don't need acts of benevolence or wondrous words to prove it to me. That's not the nature of my relationship to God.[5]

Which attitude takes more faith: To believe that God is going to miraculously take us out of all our problems and pain or to believe that God can take us *through* our trial? If your faith in God depends on seeing Him perform a miraculous healing in your life, then perhaps your faith needs some stretching.

When the leper came to Jesus for healing in Luke 5, he threw himself humbly to the ground before Jesus and prayed, "Lord, if you are willing, you can make me clean." And this must be our attitude before God as we go to Him in prayer for healing: "Lord, *if you are willing,* please heal me!" God is sovereign, and our prayers to Him must always reflect His absolute sovereignty.

Health—a state of mind?

In his book *The Call to Wholeness: Health As a Spiritual Journey,* physician Kenneth L. Bakken cites research by the American Academy of Family Physicians which shows that "two-thirds of office visits to family doctors are prompted by stress-related symptoms." He explains:

> Stress is known to be a major contributor, either directly or indirectly, to coronary heart disease, cancer, lung ailments, accidental injuries, cirrhosis of the liver and suicide—six of the leading causes of death in the United States. . . . The three most prescribed drugs in this country—Tagamet for peptic ulcers, Inderal for high blood pressure, and Valium for anxiety—offer a sad commentary on the way we have chosen to live as individuals and as a society.[6]

Norman Cousins, former editor of *Saturday Review* and noted author, wrote a book about his encounter with a massive, near-fatal heart attack, *The Healing Heart.* There he writes of the overwhelmingly important role such positive mental and emotional qualities as "hope, faith, love, laughter, and a strong will to live" had to play in his recovery. He concludes:

> A weak body becomes weaker in a mood of total surrender. The mechanisms of repair and rehabilitation that are built into the human system have a natural drive to assert themselves under conditions of illness, but that natural tendency is deferred or deflected by an erosion of the will to live, or by the absence of confidence in one's physician or in one's own ability to play a vital part in the attack on disease.

Obviously, it is absurd to suppose that there is no illness that can't be reversed. But it is also true that under conditions of extreme illness we need all the help we can get. . . . Since the human body tends to move in the direction of its expectations—plus or minus—it is important to know that attitudes of confidence and determination are no less a part of the treatment program than medical science and technology.[7]

In my book *Gold in the Making*, I told about a dear friend of mine, Diane Schmidt, and the battle she was then undergoing with cancer.[8] When the doctor first informed Diane of the diagnosis of her disease, she replied, "I want you to know, first of all, that I'm a Christian. My life is in God's hands, and I know that even if this cancer ends my life, I will live on with Him in eternity."

The doctor then listed for her the various options for treatment, the best of which seemed to be immediate surgery. She said, "That's fine, let's do the surgery." The next day, Diane was in surgery for ten hours. During that time, I waited with Diane's mother and sister. Finally the doctor came out of the operating room and said, "In all the years I've practiced medicine, I've never seen anyone face cancer with the courage and character Diane has."

Diane came through surgery and recuperation with good humor, trust in God, and a strong will to live. The doctors felt certain they had completely eliminated the cancer from her body. During and after her recovery, Diane was able to use the experience of her own cancer to encourage and minister to others who were afflicted with the disease.

Since *Gold in the Making* was published, doctors again found cancer in Diane's body, and it was spreading rapidly. Again she underwent a series of treatments, but this time the prognosis was very bad. The doctors didn't tell Diane at the time, but they felt she had only a few more months to live at most. In fact, however, she survived almost two more years. Indeed, she did far *more* than survive; she *lived* her life. Until just a short time before her death she remained actively involved in her church, in the athletic pursuits she'd always enjoyed, and in the lives of her friends.

Her doctors can only offer one explanation for the extra,

full years she was able to live: her positive, affirming, *Yes* attitude to life. She trusted God, and refused to give in to resentment or self-pity. She kept her sense of humor. Despite enormous suffering, she maintained a strong will to live, yet she was ready to die. She had peace with God. And all of these factors together enabled her to have a richer, longer life—even through the trial of terminal cancer.

Medical science is becoming increasingly aware that it's not enough to simply treat symptoms. Even in a disease of purely physiological origin, there are powerful mental, emotional, and spiritual factors that must be addressed if there is to be true healing. This truth is at the heart of the holistic approach to healing—an approach that has become something of a media fad packaged in best-selling books, touted on television talk shows, sold as big business. A fair one-line summary of extreme holistic philosophy is, "You're as healthy as you think." It is often as simplistic—and as wrong—as that.

What I'm suggesting here is an approach to health that is truly *whole*-istic. That is, we should deal with illness from the point of view that man is not merely a physical being, but a mental and spiritual being as well. We should not seek to merely cure disease, but to make people *whole*. This doesn't mean (as some holistic advocates suggest) that "health is just a state of mind." We can't forget that a virus is a *physical* organism—and so is a human being. Thus, some of our illnesses have purely physical causes, and all the "good thinking" and "positive attitude" in the world are simply powerless to prevent us from catching some of these diseases.

Kathryn Lindskoog voices concern over some of the excesses of the holistic extremists:

> Much of the insight of holistic medicine rings true because we always knew it. Is it news that we are what we eat, and we are what we think, and worry wears us out? Is it news that people die of broken hearts, that no man is an island, that the whole is more than its parts? Is it news that we are more than machines, that our bodies are the temple of the Holy Spirit, that a merry heart doeth good like medicine? Eternal news, maybe.
>
> The sick side of holistic medicine is that it promotes a blame-the-victim attitude toward people hit by serious disease.[9]

This blame-the-victim attitude usually takes the form of telling the sick person there is some direct connection between his sickness and some *sin* in his life. Certainly from a biblical point of view, *all* sickness and death is the result of original sin. As Romans 5:12 tells us, "Sin entered the world through one man [Adam], and death through sin." Too, there is sometimes a *direct* relationship between personal sin and illness. In Psalm 32, David says that when he allowed his sin to go unrepented and unconfessed, his body wasted away—a biblical expression of the relationship between the spiritual, the emotional, and the physical aspects of our being.

But sometimes there is *no* relationship between personal sins and sickness. There are moral laws operating in our world, which often cause painful consequences to follow sinful actions—but it's not as simple as $2 + 2 = 4$. In this fallen world, evil sometimes goes unpunished and good sometimes goes unrewarded.

Why, then, do we get sick?

Aside from the simple fact that our physical bodies are naturally susceptible to disease or injury, we have to understand that God sometimes chooses to *use* our illness to achieve a greater purpose. In John 9, Jesus and His disciples are passing by a man who has been blind since birth. His disciples ask Him, "Who sinned, this man or his parents, that he was born blind?" Notice the uncaring fatalism of the disciples' question, an attitude which says, "If you're sick, it's because of your sin, or your family's sin. You've gotten what you deserve from God. You'll get no help from us."

But Jesus' reply cuts through the fatalism of the disciples' question; He says that this illness is not due to anyone's sin, but "so that the work of God might be displayed in his life." Sometimes the hurt of illness strikes us so that the work of God might be displayed in our lives, so that He can make us more mature, more Christlike, or so that He can equip us to be wounded healers, able to use our pain to heal the hurts of others.

The scriptural prescription

Is God interested in our physical health? Yes, of course He is. Many of the warnings He gives us in Scripture—warnings which many people think harsh and restrictive, warnings against sexual sin or harboring anger, for example—are really God's guidelines for health. God doesn't want to hurt us. He doesn't desire our pain. In His Word, He gives us a plan for living as happy and healthy a life as possible. As surgeon Paul Brand notes,

> Scientists have verified that positive choices can have a salubrious effect on the physical body. A spirit of gratitude, inner peace, love, hope, happiness, support from friends, joy—these qualities can have far greater effect than any injection I could give. A body that is at peace and surrounded by loving support quite literally heals better. In view of this fact, the Old Testament Levitical laws and the New Testament prescriptions for spiritual health also translate into an accurate formula for physical well-being.
> The list of qualities mentioned above bears a striking parallel to the fruit of the Spirit outlined in Galatians: love, joy, peace, patience, kindness, goodness, faithfulness, gentleness, self-control. Such characteristics of growth in the Spirit can have a powerful effect on healing by properly aligning the orientation of mind and body. I am convinced that the Creator designed the mind and body to flourish when under the control of the Spirit.[10]

God *does* care about our physical health—but He cares even *more* about our spiritual health, our maturity, our growth, because these add up to *eternal* health, a quality of wholeness that lasts long after the physical body has fallen to dust. God is sovereign, and I cannot demand that He give me a life of health or comfort or success if that is not His choice. It has taken my whole life to learn that truth—and I'm still learning it.

I have to confess that until a few years ago the sovereignty of God was little more than just another doctrine to me. But I have known a man to whom the sovereignty of God was not just a doctrine, but the passion and obsession of his life—and I want to share with you something of what he taught me.

Two ways to live on

I came to know Rev. Theodore Lyons in early 1983, when he joined the pastoral staff of our church. During that year, he became a close friend, and even a spiritual father to me. At sixty-four, Ted was a wise, generous man with a warm sense of humor and humility. I also came to know him as a man of courage, a man who was battling cancer.

Ted staked his life on the claim of Romans 8:28–29: "And we know that God causes all things to work together for good to those who love God, to those who are called according to his purpose. For whom he foreknew, he also predestined to be conformed to the image of his Son" (NASB). Christlikeness was the goal of Ted's life. He understood that God in His sovereign wisdom could use even the ravages of cancer to accomplish His good.

We talked together of this truth during the final weeks of Ted's life. He was lying in his hospital bed and tears were welling in his eyes as he told me, "I'm just trusting in Romans 8:28 and 29, Ron, and however God wants to work out the details is okay with me." I knew he was telling the truth, but I knew it was a hard truth. I knew he was in terrible pain, and that it hurt him deeply to know he was scheduled very soon to leave his wife, his three children, and his many friends who would remain behind. And yet, despite the pain and grief he felt, there shone through it all an amazing confidence and assurance in his Lord.

Throughout his battle with cancer, Ted used his suffering to discover his identification with Christ. "Ron," he once told me, "this cancer is teaching me just a little bit more about the suffering and humiliation of Christ on the Cross." Through his pain, Ted was becoming more and more like Christ. The process continued day by day throughout his illness, right up until that moment on a sunny autumn morning in 1983 when God called Ted Lyons home to be with Him.

There are two ways that a Christian lives on after death. One way is by living on in eternity with Jesus. The other way is by living on through the lives of those in whom we have invested ourselves—those we've encouraged, affirmed, and built up to be like Christ. Ted lives on in both of these ways. Today, he is healed and free from pain, a joint-heir with Christ in eternity. But he also lives on in me and in many other people he taught and encouraged through his example.

Don't you want to live and die like that? Don't you want

to live on and on, both in eternity and in the lives of others around you?

God doesn't always engineer miraculous physical cures in our lives. He never promised to. This is a hard truth—but it's also a glorious truth, because we know He is able to bring about even *greater* miracles of true healing—healing of the spirit, healing of the soul, healing of others—even through the tough process of our deepest pain.

3

Healing the Hurt
of Loss

God mourns with us. He sits down beside us and mingles His tears with ours.

—Theodore Lyons

Just as the sufferings of Christ flow over into our lives, so also through Christ our comfort overflows.

—2 Corinthians 1:5

If you were to walk into my office and look at my desk, you would find (somewhere amid the clutter) a polished rock. It's not a gemstone by any means, yet to me it's very precious. My office is filled with mementos and reminders, and this bright and shiny rock is a reminder of a boy name Corey.

About seven years ago, my wife Shirley and I had the opportunity to go to Austin, Texas, where I spoke during a week of meetings at the church pastored by my friend, Gary Dennis. We stayed with Gary and Sarah Dennis, and during every spare moment I would go outside with their eight-year-old boy, Corey. We talked, laughed, and played ball together. In that short week we built up a great friendship. I remember telling Shirley at the time, "Corey is the greatest little guy! What a joy he must be to his mom and dad."

When it was time for us to go, Corey's tears just rolled down his face. It hurt me to say good-bye to him. At the last moment before we pulled away, Corey dashed into the house. Moments later, he came back outside with a small polished rock in his hands. "Oh, that's Corey's favorite rock!" said Sarah, as Corey placed his precious gift in my hands— the polished rock I keep on my desk to this day.

One Friday night a few years ago, we received word that Corey Dennis had died of cancer at the tender age of eleven. All human life is short. It hangs by a slender thread. The loss of a loved one may come at any time. And when it comes, the trial of loss stabs us deeply. Loss touches our lives in many ways. It may come through the death of a loved one, but the pain of loss often comes to us in other ways as well.

In 1963, Brian Sternberg was named Outstanding Athlete of the Year by several sports periodicals. He held the world record for the pole vault at 16′ 8″. As part of the intense training he was undergoing for a dual track and field competition between the United States and the Soviet Union, Brian was working out on a trampoline. A split-second's misjudgment brought him down the wrong way, injuring his spine. From that instant on, Brian has been paralyzed from the neck down.

Brian continues to live with almost intolerable pain every day of his life. At a Fellowship of Christian Athletes conference a few years ago, I saw a crowd of young athletes weep openly as they listened to the testimony of Brian Sternberg, speaking from his wheelchair about the love of Jesus Christ that he has experienced—even through the tragedy of his loss of health.

Brian once told me that his favorite passage of Scripture was Philippians 3:7–8—"Whatever was to my profit I now consider loss for the sake of Christ. What is more, I consider everything a loss compared to the surpassing greatness of knowing Christ Jesus my Lord, for whose sake I have lost all things. I consider them rubbish, that I may gain Christ." As a deeply committed and competitive athlete, Brian prized his health and vitality above almost everything else in life. He hates his paralysis. He doesn't understand why God would allow such a trial of loss in his life. Yet, compared with the surpassing greatness of knowing Christ, Brian Sternberg is learning to write off everything he once had, including his health, as a *loss*.

Some of us experience the hurt of loss in the area of our finances and material security. Mr. Foster was a friend of mine, an executive of a major corporation in the Midwest. He was a respected and successful family man. But as he ascended the corporate ladder, he began to learn more and more about the way his company operated, with unethical and often illegal practices toward employees, clients, and the government.

Because Mr. Foster sought to live his entire life under the lordship of Jesus Christ, he realized he could not be a part of the highly placed corruption in his company, nor could he remain silent about what was happening around him. So he began to challenge those illicit practices—and it was made clear that he would have to "play ball" or face removal. So Mr. Foster resigned. He lost his job, his handsome salary and benefits, his pension, and his financial security during a time when jobs were hard to come by. But in the midst of this deep loss, he had maintained his integrity.

John White, in his book *The Golden Cow,* observes that Jesus calls all of His followers to this same kind of self-sacrificing integrity. He explains:

> To give up everything for Christ consists of an *internal* relinquishment of all our possessions. . . . All of us are to have a contract with Christ that whenever obedience to Him means sacrifice of any degree, even to losing everything we have or to facing prison and death, then obedience is what matters. The obedience will be all the easier if we daily relinquish to Him all we possess.
>
> All Christians are called to be disciples. All Christians at any time, under any circumstances, are to be ready for new sets of instructions from headquarters which might mean total material loss.[1]

Some of us face loss in the form of lost hopes and dreams. This was the hurt of loss suffered by George Matheson, a young man living in the mid-1800s. Afflicted by an incurable disorder that gradually robbed him of his sight, Matheson found himself increasingly avoided by family and friends. Finally, there was only one person who stood by him: his fiancée.

But as the day of their wedding grew closer, she began to be less affectionate, less spontaneous with Matheson. He knew something was troubling her, so he asked her what was wrong. At first she said nothing, then, with her own beautiful eyes averted from his gradually failing eyes, she blurted, "I'm sorry. I just can't face a future of caring for a blind man." With that, she left him—forever.

George Matheson had lost his sight, his friends, his family, and the love of the only woman he ever cared for. All his plans and dreams for the future were dashed. And it was in the depths of this terrible loss that Matheson sat down at his desk and wrote the lines of that great hymn,

O Love that will not let me go,
I rest my weary soul in Thee;
I give Thee back the life I owe,
That in Thine ocean depths its flow
May richer, fuller be.

Because the hurt of loss can come into our lives in so many ways, I want to broaden the definition of loss beyond the experience of losing a loved one. We experience the pain of loss when friends and family members move to a distant city. We feel loss when we reach a realization that some lifelong goal or ambition will never be fulfilled. We know the hurt of loss as we grow older and our health and vitality begin to wane. We suffer a loss as deep and painful as the death of a loved one when our marriage begins to break down.

Holding on—loosely

"Life is like an onion," wrote Carl Sandburg. "You peel it off one layer at a time, and sometimes you weep." That's a great truth: in life, sometimes you weep. The problem is, deep down, most of us really don't believe it. We tend to see life as an idealized journey of our own making, without any hills or unexpected turns. We plan for the future and we build up unrealistic expectations of what life should be like. Deep down, we all expect to keep our health, our loved ones, and our possessions throughout our lives.

But loss is inevitable in life. We don't anticipate that fact; we don't even want to think about it. We fool ourselves into believing we have every right to expect a life without loss— and so we begin to take life and health and loved ones for granted.

Before my brother Paul became ill, I never gave much thought to the possibility I might lose him so soon. The urgency of the diagnosis of cancer focused and concentrated my mind on my relationship with Paul, and indeed on all my relationships with family and friends. Since then, every meal I take with my family is like a sacrament to me, a holy meal. But I often wonder, why did it take having to face the loss of my brother before I stopped taking him for granted, before those daily moments with my family became so precious?

I don't ever want to take life and the ones I love for granted. I don't ever want to live my life as if it's just another day. I want to keep gaining more of God's perspective on the *gift* of life we have as we share it with the ones we love.

But there's a paradox here. For while we need to gain a deeper appreciation of God's gifts to us, He never intended for us to clutch them to ourselves. All God's gifts are for us to enjoy and to care for while we have them—but a time will come when God will have them back.

Corrie ten Boom was fond of saying, "I have learned to hold on to everything loosely." That has been hard for me in the loss of my brother, and in the loss of my father and so many close friends over the years. It's not easy for me to hold loosely the ones I love deeply, and I'm certain it's not easy for you either. But I am slowly learning that the hurt of loss calls us to a response: Will we simply resent our loss as a great unfairness—or will we be open to God's sustaining grace so that we can *grow* through the hurt of loss?

God's truth for our lives often springs at us unbidden, delivered in a package we are unwilling to receive. It's only natural to want to reject the *pain* of loss, but by God's grace we can make the healing choice to accept the *lessons* of loss. As Benjamin Franklin said, "Those things that hurt, instruct." Similarly, Paul in Romans 5 tells us, "Suffering produces perseverance; perseverance, character; and character, hope." As followers of Christ, we want to gain all the lessons and growth to be found in our trial of loss—or else we will have suffered for nothing.

C. S. Lewis understood very well the hurt of loss. Almost every book he wrote is a pleasure to read, but there is one book by C. S. Lewis that is filled with pain and questioning. In *A Grief Observed,* Lewis bluntly recorded his feelings of anguish over the loss of his wife to cancer. "Her absence is like the sky," he wrote, "spread over everything." [2] And, "Where is God? . . . Go to Him when your need is desperate, when all other help is vain, and what do you find? A door slammed in your face, and a sound of bolting and double bolting on the inside. After that, silence." [3] For Lewis, it was many months before the silence ended and he was able to hear God's voice again.

Let's not kid ourselves: the hurt of loss is universal. While the Christian has the blessed assurance of God's presence in times of loss, the *pain* of loss afflicts Christians and non-Christians alike. If we're honest, we have to confess that our times of loss are often times of questioning, of anger, as we demand of God, *Why?* C. S. Lewis recorded all these emotions and painful questions in *A Grief Observed* —yet he ultimately came to a place of acceptance of his loss. So may you and I.

Martin Luther was a great man of faith: the founder of the Protestant Reformation, the author of the powerful hymn "A Mighty Fortress Is Our God." Yet when Luther's beautiful fourteen-year-old daughter Magdalena died, Luther was torn by a despairing sense of loss. Almost as troubling to Luther as his grief was the fact that he was unable to set aside the normal human reaction to loss. To him, the loss of a daughter became a crisis of faith. "How strange it is to know that Magdalena is at peace, and all is well," he said, "and yet to be so sorrowful!"

Luther went through many long months of depression, questioning, and inner struggle. He wrestled deeply with the pain of his loss. But Luther ultimately emerged from his struggle with a deeper understanding of how a father's love for a child is like our Father's love for us.

Maturity in Christ does not enable us to feel the hurt of loss less keenly. We are human, and so we will grieve. This is why Paul writes, "Brothers, we do not want you to . . . grieve like the rest of men, who have no hope" (1 Thess. 4:13). He acknowledges that, yes, we will grieve—but *not* like those who have no hope! The Christian experience of loss does not entail absence of sorrow, but of *hopeless* sorrow.

Our hope is Christ, who wept in grief over the loss of his friend Lazarus. And our hope is in God the loving Father, who has known the death of His only Son. God knows the hurt of mourning, and He mingles His tears with our own. His grief sanctifies our own human sorrow.

Responding to loss

No one can go through an experience of loss unchanged. Whether our hurt is due to the loss of a loved one, a loss of health, a financial loss, or some other cause, this trial will inevitably produce a set of responses within us. The first response will be a normal, human reaction, involving some combination of shock, denial, anger, guilt, and depression. There is nothing sinful or unhealthy about such a reaction to loss. However, if this initial reaction is not worked through, it can deepen into a lifetime of bitterness. So it's very important that we make the healing choice to couple our normal *human reaction* with a *divine reaction*.

The divine reaction enables us, after a normal period of pain and grief, to say to God, "I accept this loss in my life. While I may not understand it, I submit to it. While it's painful, I see it as reality. Lord, please teach me your lesson in this loss, and help me to grow more like Christ because of it." That's not a natural response; it's a *supernatural* response, and it's the kind of response God ultimately wants to achieve in us.

This is a supernatural reaction because it goes completely against the way we feel. The hurt of loss is still there—but as we open ourselves to what God wants to teach us in our hurt, the pain takes on the nature of a healing act of surgery, not merely a scarring wound.

A truly deep loss—the loss of someone close to you or the breakdown of a marriage relationship—is going to hurt for a long time. And even after the pain has subsided, and you are able to get on with your life again, there will be moments when the pain will come back, seemingly as deep and sharp as the first moment it was inflicted. Expect the grief process to take time. Don't let it throw you; you're going to come through.

The grief process took a long time for Job. Here was a man who had everything—and lost it all. At the beginning of the book of Job, he is pictured as an amazingly rich man—rich in many ways. He is described, first of all, as "blameless and upright; he feared God and shunned evil." In other words, Job was a genuinely authentic man of God, rich in spiritual assets. And he had seven sons and three daughters; Job was rich in family. He had enormous holdings of land, livestock, and servants; Job was rich in possessions. He was, according to Job 1:3, "the greatest man among all the people of the East"; Job was rich in reputation and respect.

But this godly, respected, affluent man was soon to be plunged head-to-heels into the deepest trial of loss anyone could possibly imagine. Job's losses came suddenly and mounted rapidly. First, enemies attacked his fields, slaughtering servants and stealing oxen and donkeys. A fire from the sky destroyed his sheep-flocks and killed more servants. Next came the loss of his camels and the rest of his servants. Finally Job's ten children and oldest brother were killed.

One moment, Job was "the greatest man among all the people of the East." The next moment, he was bereaved of almost all his family. He was financially wiped out. Notice, too, that Job's trial was not the result of any wrongdoing in his life. He was blameless before God. The losses Job suffered were enormously unfair.

How, then, did Job respond? Job 1:20 records, "At this, Job got up and tore his robe and shaved his head. Then he fell to the ground in worship." Job reacted, first, with grief. That's a normal, human response. Job was not stoically indifferent to his loss, nor did he take masochistic pleasure in it. He grieved, and he displayed his grief openly.

But then Job went a step further. He coupled his normal, human response with a *divine* response: he *worshiped.* He bowed his face to the ground in a gesture of adoration toward his God. And in Job 1:21 he demonstrates a divine response to loss still further, saying, "Naked I came from my mother's womb, and naked I will depart. The Lord gave and the Lord has taken away; may the name of the Lord be praised." This incredibly rich man had learned to hold on to everything loosely.

And Job 1:22 adds, "In all this, Job did not sin by charging God with wrongdoing." Reading this, we might think, "Well, that's Job. He was some kind of super-saint, a legendary man of God." But no, he was simply a human being who had made a choice to so closely link himself to God that he didn't get derailed by the hard places of life. In *Pain's Hidden Purpose,* Don Baker observes,

Screaming "ouch" when you stub your toe is not cursing God.

One of the tragic interpretations of Job has encouraged people to suffer in silence. It has heaped guilt upon them when they dared to ask God a question or to suggest to God that they would like some relief. . . . Tears are therapeutic and talk is therapeutic. God has given us tear ducts and tongues, and they become a very real part of the relief process when we hurt. And Job employed both.[4]

The message of Job is not, "Here is a legendary saint of unattainable faith," but, "Here is a flesh-and-blood man who knew deep trouble, and he ultimately responded with God's perspective." Job coupled his human reaction to a divine reaction: he *wept* and he *worshiped*. That's a choice you and I can make as well, no matter how the hurt of loss touches our lives.

On the ash heap

What more could happen to Job?

But more *did* happen. Job 2 records that he was afflicted "with painful sores from the soles of his feet to the top of his head." Job experienced the loss of his health. At this point his wife turned against him in rage. "Are you still holding on to your faith in God?" she cried. "Why don't you just curse God and die?" Job then found himself shut out of his house and left to die on a heap of ashes, the ancient equivalent of a garbage dump. There, amid the filth and flies, he picked up a shard of broken pottery, shook the dust from it, and began to scrape the accumulating corruption from his stinging flesh. At this point Job became the most miserable and degraded man on earth.

Then three of Job's friends—Eliphaz, Bildad, and Zophar—heard of Job's troubles and made the journey to offer him comfort. Approaching him, they found him a disfigured, disease-ridden derelict sprawled on an ash heap at the edge of town. Immediately they cried out, tore their robes, and wept over him. Then they sat on the ground with him for seven days and seven nights. For a whole week, no one said a word to him, not even to quote Scripture. They simply offered the comfort of their presence. If only they had left it at that.

But at the end of that week, Job's friends began to offer "advice"—and at that point they ceased to be of any further comfort to Job. Eliphaz and Bildad accused Job of hiding sin in his life. When Job protested his innocence, Zophar presumptuously claimed to speak for God, calling Job a liar. Finally Job cried out in frustration, "Miserable comforters are you all! Will your long-winded speeches never end?"

Here is a sharply etched illustration of two ways to stand by people in a time of loss: one, a ministry of quiet presence with the sufferer; the other, a reckless and judgmental intrusion into the sufferer's misery. When someone is going through a trial, he probably doesn't need to hear more words, not even words from the Bible. He just needs a friend who will offer simple presence and practical encouragement. In God's own time, he may gain a divine perspective on his trial, but that perspective can never be imposed on him from without, especially during the very worst depths of his suffering.

Loss transformed

At the conclusion of his time of trial, Job is able to say, "My ears had heard of you but now my eyes have seen you" (Job 42:5). In other words, Job was saying that before his trial of deep loss he had only heard of God—but now, with his own eyes, he had seen God powerfully working in his life. That's what the hurt of loss often does to our lives: our trials enable us to see God in new and meaningful ways. All the things we've heard about God, all the doctrines and sermons and books about God are completely transcended by the reality of God's presence through our pain and loss—and we emerge from our trials with the knowledge that we have seen Him at work with our very own eyes.

In so many ways, we discover that God is able to take our trial of loss and radically transform it. This happened in a tangible way in Job's life: "The Lord made him prosperous again and gave him twice as much as he had before" (Job 42:10). Yet this verse is being misused and distorted in many quarters of the church today. God doesn't promise that if you lose a $20,000-a-year job this month, then he'll give you a $40,000-a-year job next month. The way God transforms our loss is up to Him, not us.

God's blessings are not always material blessings. He often takes what is tangible and gives what is intangible: deeper faith, stronger character, compassion for others, and peace that passes human understanding.

Why?

A young woman, only eighteen years old, was driving alone on the freeway, headed back to college after a visit home with her family. On the way, she ran into mechanical trouble, carefully pulled as far off the pavement as she could, then got out of her car to open the trunk. Just then, a drunk driver steered his car over the center divider of the freeway, across several lanes of traffic, and directly toward the unsuspecting young woman. In an instant, her life was over.

"We prayed together as a family the night before she left," this young woman's father told me. "We prayed *specifically* that God would protect our daughter, but He *didn't!* And I want to know why! If God is all-loving and all-powerful, He could have deflected the path of that car just eighteen inches, and my daughter would be alive today! *Why* didn't He?"

I don't know why. Certainly, there are *partial* answers, such as the fact that this drunk driver's actions were a matter of human free will, not an act of God—yet such philosophical niceties mean little in the face of real human tragedy. The fact is that a father's prayer was answered *No*, and if we're honest with ourselves we have to echo this father's haunting question: *Why?* Indeed, faced with God's mysterious *No* to our prayers, we may well be tempted to cry out, "Why, then, should we pray? If we are powerless to influence God's actions and to obtain His protection for our lives and loved ones through prayer, then *why pray at all?*"

I want to encourage you not to despair in the face of God's unsearchable *No*. I can testify that a prayer prayed humbly before God is the positive power to change things, to move mountains, to radically alter lives. I've seen many situations when the only thing that stood between life and death, success or failure, salvation or hell, was the prayer of one of God's faithful servants.

At the same time, we have to concede that it's the One who *answers* prayer—not the one who prays—who is sovereign. God's will is not always going to coincide with our will.

Sometimes God must allow us to be hurt in order for us to be healed, and our only assurance at such times is the fact that God is sovereign. When His will has been made clear to us, and His will is clearly not our will, His way not our way, then we must pray anew, asking God to teach us His lesson through our trial of loss.

One hymnwriter put it this way:

> *What He takes and what He gives us*
> *Shows how precious His love is for us.*

Notice, the author of these lines had the courage to write "what He takes" first. It's true. Very often, it is what He *takes* from us that shows how precious His love is for us. That's the lesson of a lifetime—a lifetime spent seeking God's perspective on the hurt of loss.

It's terrible to go through the tragedy of a loss, but it's even more terrible to suffer the hurt of loss and not even learn anything from it. In the final analysis, life is a process of learning and preparation. We are preparing ourselves for that one form of loss we all face: the loss of our earthly lives, by which we will one day gain all of eternity.

4

Healing the Hurt of Loneliness

Alone, alone, all, all alone.
Alone on a wide, wide sea.
—Samuel Taylor Coleridge

I will be with you always.
—Jesus Christ, Matthew 28:20

Rupert Brooke—that great, sad poet of England who died in World War I—was a very lonely man. One day, Brooke boarded a steamship sailing from Liverpool to New York City. He stood at the rail, surrounded by throngs of people—but totally alone. There was no one to say good-bye or shed a tear.

On an impulse, Brooke left the rail and ran down the gangplank. On the dock he found a young boy about ten years old. He knelt and looked the boy in the eyes and asked, "Young man, would you like to earn sixpence?"

"Indeed I would, sir!" said the boy.

Brooke took some coins from his pocket and pressed them into the boy's hand. "Then, lad," he said, "would you wave to me as the boat goes out to sea?"

Alone.

It's perhaps the most desolate word in the world. You can't buy your way out of loneliness. You can't wish it away. "Loneliness," as Thomas Wolfe observed, "far from being a rare and curious phenomenon peculiar to myself and a few other solitary men, is the central fact of human existence."

Every human being of every age and culture, says psychologist Erich Fromm, is confronted with one question: "How to overcome separateness, how to achieve union, how to transcend one's own individual life and find at-onement." He explains,

Man is gifted with . . . awareness of himself, of his fellow man, of his past, and of the possibilities of his future. This awareness of himself as a separate entity, the awareness of his own short life span, of the fac* that without his will he is born and against his will he dies, that he will die before those whom he loves, or they before him, the awareness of his aloneness and separateness, of his helplessness before the forces of nature and of society, all this makes his separate disunited existence an unbearable prison. . . .

The deepest need of man, then, is the need to overcome his separateness, to leave the prison of his aloneness.[1]

Here is a surgically precise diagnosis of the loneliness of the human condition—a condition to which Jesus Himself was no stranger. From the cross He cried out one of the most stark expressions of loneliness and alienation ever uttered: "My God! My God! Why have you forsaken me?" Jesus, the Son of God, was alone, separated from God the Father as the moment of His death approached. There He took our deepest hurt of loneliness and crucified it forever. The "at-onement" that Erich Fromm said every human being seeks is found through the *atonement* Christ purchased for us on the Cross.

In Revelation 3:20, Jesus says, "Here I am! I stand at the door and knock. If anyone hears my voice and opens the door, I will go in and eat with him, and he with me." Jesus waits outside the door of your heart, wanting nothing more than to come in with you, break bread with you, and end your loneliness.

Death by loneliness

Everyone knows the terrible 3 A.M. loneliness that comes with insomnia, often mixed with worry about the problems of the day or the dread of death. The shadows of our fears loom especially large in the middle of the night, when we have no one to talk to.

But loneliness doesn't come only in the pit of night or in times of solitude. The hurt of loneliness often stabs us when we are surrounded by people. As Lloyd Ogilvie observes,

> Loneliness . . . lurks under many a jolly mask, and pulses in the hearts of the most gregarious and outgoing. It's there beneath the busy adequacy or pretended assurance of the popular, the famous, and the attractive people we admire.
>
> One of the most crucial discoveries I have made over the years, working with and listening to people, is that loneliness has little to do with the absence of people. We can feel lonely in a crowd, among friends, in a marriage, in the family, at a sorority or fraternity house, and in a church.[2]

I met Helen at the back of the church following the worship service. She accepted my hand, smiled bashfully, and nodded as I greeted her. I chatted with her for a few moments, but she volunteered very little information about herself. She hardly said anything unless encouraged to speak. She was obviously a very lonely woman.

Helen continued coming to church. My wife and I invited her into our home several times, and I slowly began to learn more about her. She had no family and no close friends. She liked coming to church because the people there were friendly. They smiled, she said, and many spoke to her.

I tried to help Helen find a group where she could experience deeper Christian fellowship than she was receiving on Sunday mornings. But she just didn't seem to connect with any of the groups in our church.

One evening, just a few days before Christmas, Helen was found dead in her small downtown apartment. In one desolate act, completely alone, Helen had taken her life. Seven people, including myself, stood at the graveside as the plain wooden box was lowered into the earth. Though some of us had tried, none of us had really gotten to know Helen very well.

Since then, I've often asked myself, Why? How could a woman die of loneliness in a church filled with joyful, outgoing Christians?

And yet I believe Helen's tragedy is not really so unusual after all. Surely, the marks of a lonely soul were very plain on her life and death; most of us keep our loneliness—and, indeed, all our deepest feelings—hidden from view. Not many people will act on their feelings of loneliness as Helen did— but there are many lonely people in every church, and each is a silent tragedy.

An epidemic of loneliness

In 1983, the California State Department of Mental Health studied seven thousand adults from ages thirty to fifty-nine. One of the dynamics under investigation in this study was the correlation between *friendship* and *health*. The researchers found that people without long-term friendships have from two to five times the normal mortality rate for their age group, and experienced higher than normal incidences of cancer, heart disease, circulatory disease, and other ailments.

Certainly, that is not to say that people with few friends will inevitably get sick, or that those with deep friendships are immune from illness; there are many factors that contribute to the state of our health, either good or ill. But this study does seem to establish a statistical connection between loneliness and a tendency toward decreased health and vitality.

At the same time, we are increasingly becoming a nation of strangers—rootless, friendless, and alienated. This is the age of modular relationships and disposable people. The average American moves fourteen times in a lifetime, uprooting acquaintances before they have a chance to blossom into friendships. Loneliness is an epidemic. It's stealing our happiness. It's even *killing* us—silently and slowly as it steals our health, or swiftly and shockingly, as it killed Helen.

A *Newsweek* report following the death of actor William Holden began, "William Holden was a very private man, and he died a very private death. Alone in his apartment in Santa Monica, California, he bled to death from a gash in his forehead caused by a drunken fall against his bedside table. It was four or five days later that his body was found." [3] Holden's films had captivated millions of viewers for decades—yet when he died, four or five days passed and no one even missed him. Why? The closing lines of the article suggest a possible reason: "Holden guarded his privacy with increasing vigilance." A fitting analogy, I think, for many of us.

Why are so many Christians dying inside, even though surrounded by other Christians? One reason, perhaps, is self-imposed isolation—not physical isolation, perhaps, but distance and guardedness in our relationships with one another. We vigilantly guard our privacy. We're afraid to let anyone into our lives. We smile because we're expected to smile, and behind the smile our loneliness deepens. And it will continue to deepen until we make the healing choice to become transparent to a few trusted friends, to let ourselves be known.

No one can exist in a vacuum. In Genesis 2:18, God said, "It is not good for man to be alone." That's why God gave Adam, the first lonely man, a *family*. And God has given you and me a family as well. Even if you have no spouse, no parents, and no children, you have a family indeed, and that family is the church.

Biblically, the church is not a building or an institution or a religious organization. The church is to be our Family of Faith, a place of healing, belonging, and joy. Have you found your place in the Family of Faith? I don't just mean a church to attend on Sunday mornings, but a place to truly *share your life*—your hurts, your doubts, your fears, your joys—with a few other Christians.

Walking in the light

In John 3:21, Jesus commands us to live not only righteously, but *openly,* to "live by the truth," to "come into the light" so that our lives and deeds may be known. First John 1:7 tells us that "if we walk in the light" then "we have fellowship with one another." The Christian who chooses privacy and isolation from deep relationships, who chooses self-reliance and self-sufficiency, has chosen *darkness* and *loneliness.* Isolation is the black hole of the soul; withdrawal from vulnerable, open relationships will suck all the light and warmth out of your life.

In *There's a Lot More to Health Than Not Being Sick,* Bruce Larson confronts us with the question, "How are you fixed for friends?" He writes:

The question "How are you fixed for friends?" could be phrased in more psychological or spiritual terms. You could ask, "Is there a group of people to which you really belong?" or, "Are there people who know you totally, warts and all?" or, "Do you need to account for yourself, your time to anyone else?" The point is that it is hard to be a whole person without at least a few friends with whom you are free to be yourself, to whom you are accountable. To know and to be known is a vital ingredient for physical and spiritual wholeness.[4]

That's how the Family of Faith functions in the life of the individual who chooses belonging over aloneness, community over isolation, light over darkness. Our fellow Christians let us truly be ourselves, affirming us in an atmosphere of unconditional acceptance. At the same time, they watch our lives and help us to become more like Christ, supporting us in prayer and opening their lives to us.

For me, all of this takes place in several ways, but especially in a setting which, in our church, we call "house churches." We meet in homes, study the Bible together, apply the truth of the Bible to our lives, openly share our joys and sorrows with each other, and uphold each other in prayer. In my own house church there have been people of different ages, background, education, and economic status; people struggling with unemployment, marital stresses, the pain of divorce, guilt and doubt, financial problems, and the loss of loved ones. Whatever our individual differences, we have learned one thing together: the ground is level at the foot of the Cross. We all struggle and hurt—and we all need each other.

In my role as a pastor, I continually lead meetings and counsel other people. In my house church, however, I'm just another fellow-struggler. For a couple of hours a week, I don't have to lead; I can simply *belong*. I can ask others to counsel me, to pray for me, to forgive me, and to hold me accountable. Close Christian community in small groups of caring, Scripture study and prayer is the best way to transcend the lostness we often feel in our churches, large or small.

A few years ago, a young friend of mine called me on the phone. His voice quavered as he told me that his girlfriend had suddenly broken up with him. She had dropped out of school, left the church she was attending, and joined a cult. "You know, Ron," he told me, "the thing that's so amazing is that she can't even explain to me what the cult believes."

"Well, do you know why she joined?" I asked.

"She said she joined because she found a kind of acceptance and caring in this cult that she never experienced in her church—and now she's not lonely anymore."

The cults are beating us at our own game! They've discovered a distinctive dynamic that the twentieth century church has largely lost, but which *energized* the life of the early New Testament church: intense community and fellowship. When Christians in the first century church said "fellowship" (*koinonia* in New Testament Greek), they meant the disclosure of the deep recesses of their lives to other believers, sharing their possessions with others in need, and celebrating together in prayer, praise, and worship. This same kind of *koinonia*-fellowship can be ours today as we begin to walk together in the light, sharing our lives together, confessing our hurts and failures to one another, and *liberating* each other from loneliness.

Making connection

Some time ago, AT&T, the nation's largest long-distance telephone company, spent $60 million dollars to find just the right phrase to move people out of their chairs and over to the phone to make a long-distance call. The result of all this expensive research, testing, and creative development was a simple five-word slogan:

Reach out and touch someone.

Everyone knows these familiar commercials, with their scenes of distant loved ones making connection across the miles, old friends reminiscing and sharing their deepest feelings, parents telling their kids they're sorry for some thoughtless outburst, and kids telling their parents, "Hey, that's okay." And each of these scenes is tagged, *Reach out and touch someone.*

I admit it: I'm a pushover for these commercials. Why do they manipulate our emotions so effectively? Because they touch a real longing in each of us to be reached, to be touched, to be known deep within. These commercials offer *connection* and *intimacy* with someone outside of ourselves. They offer an instant bridging of the distance between two people. The underlying message of all these mini-dramas is that the cure for loneliness is just a phone call away.

Reach out and touch someone. This would be an excellent

slogan for the church, for any church, even though AT&T thought of it first. How are we doing at the job of reaching out, touching human need with the love of Christ, and helping lonely people feel less alone?

I made a surprising discovery a few years ago. I found that roughly *half* of all adults who joined our church during one given year were single—either unmarried, widowed, or divorced. In fact, this trend is really indicative of the American church at large.

Yet at the same time, we are seeing the emergence of some very hurtful and unbiblical teaching regarding single people in the church. Let me quote the recent words of two leading Bible teachers. One wrote, "Since the family is the place where God ultimately builds character, you will never become fully mature in Christ so long as you are unmarried." The other said, "If you are unmarried, you are incomplete."

Frankly, I get angry when I hear statements such as these—not only because they are unbiblical, but because they assign a kind of second-class status to unmarried Christians, a view the Bible never endorses. And such statements inflict greater pain on people who have already been hurt by life, people who struggle with the pain of loneliness.

Paul, writing in 1 Corinthians 7, states that the single condition, far from being any kind of second-class status, is a *special* condition. He says of the unmarried that "it is good for them to stay unmarried, as I am." In verses 32–35, Paul states that there is a definite benefit for those who are single, in terms of their service for Jesus Christ: their interests are undivided; they do not have to be burdened with the problems of caring for a family; they can serve the Lord with undivided devotion.

Some people think there could be nothing worse than remaining single for life—but there is: being married to the *wrong* person for life. John Denver's beautiful, evocative song, "Seasons of the Heart," tells of a husband and wife who have been together for many years, and yet have become strangers to each other. One sad line in the song tells it all: "When I'm lying right beside you is when I feel the most alone of all." Marriage is no cure for loneliness. Some of the loneliest people in the world are married people.

Yet I don't want to be misunderstood: Marriage is a beautiful gift of God. I don't want to downgrade marriage, but to upgrade the status of single Christians. Everyone in the church has first-class status in the kingdom of God. If you're single, don't wonder why you've missed God's best for your life; rejoice that you *have* God's best, and then use your gift of singleness for God's glory.

Victims of divorce

In 1 Timothy 5:3, Paul tells us we are to give special honor and concern to those who are bereaved. And I believe Paul has given us a principle here that applies not only to those who have been widowed, but to divorced Christians as well. Psychologists tell us that the depth of sorrow that accompanies divorce is second only to that which accompanies the death of a loved one. That pain is often compounded by the ordeal of court trials, the bitterness and anger of spouse vs. spouse recriminations, and the self-righteous accusations and judgments of many in the church.

People often quote verses such as Malachi 2:16, " 'I hate divorce,' says the Lord God," seemingly unaware that it's divorce itself—not divorced *people*—he hates. God hates divorce because it's such a tragic and destructive thing in human lives. But God unconditionally loves *people,* including divorced people. It's true that people often enter into divorce for sinful reasons, such as selfishness, infidelity, or lack of commitment. But many people are truly *victims* of divorce—people who have been abused and discarded by an uncaring or hostile spouse.

The victims of divorce have gone through years of misery in an unhappy marriage. Now they're alone and seeking to rebuild their lives. They've been told by their spouse that they're unwanted. Their self-esteem has been cruelly wounded. Now they come to the church and just ask for a place of belonging and refuge, and maybe just a friend or two to say, "You're going to be all right. We're your friends and we're going to help you get better."

But how does the church all too often respond? "Divorced? Sorry, you're all washed up. You're second-class." I've seen it happen again and again: people who have been victimized once by divorce are made victims again—victims of self-righteous, unloving people in the church.

People who have just experienced the sorrow of either divorce or bereavement have a long process ahead of them. There is an authentic, long-term grief process—and we need to be sensitive to that process as we stand by the victims of loss or divorce. But grief also has a tendency to turn to a kind of destructive self-pity in the life of a lonely person if he or she is never directed outward, toward God, toward others, away from self. Today there is a growing convergence of agreement on this biblical truth among physicians, psychologists, sociologists, and theologians.

The apostle Paul understood this fact well. He knew that only a cause greater than ourselves can ever truly rid us of loneliness. So he established a plan to care for the needs of those who were alone—in particular, for widows—in the early church. We see that plan in 1 Timothy 5:3–16, where Paul outlines the duties and qualifications of a special order or registry of widows who were cared for by the early church, and who in turn were given responsibility for a ministry of service in the church. You see, Paul was a master psychologist. He was well aware of the tremendous therapeutic value that Christian *servanthood* can have when someone is going through grief and loneliness.

Hundreds of times, I've heard statements like: "I've got to become whole first; I've got to get rid of this loneliness first. *Then* I'll serve." I've found that statement almost always *not* to be true. Certainly it may be true for people with especially deep emotional problems. And certainly the person who has recently suffered a deep loss or trial will need some time to heal before getting back into active service. But I'm convinced that, in general, the therapy for loneliness is to get *out* of yourself, to lose yourself in service to God and others. The self-fulfillment philosophy of our culture says, "Get into yourself, get in touch with yourself, fulfill yourself." This philosophy saws across the grain of the Christian gospel.

There's one saying of Christ which is recorded in all four Gospels: "Whoever finds his life will lose it, and whoever loses his life for my sake will find it." I've seen the truth of that statement proved again and again: those who introspectively try to "find" themselves, who try to get "into" themselves, almost always end up sinking deeper into alienation, emotional turmoil, and loneliness. But those who get out of themselves and lose themselves in service to Christ and others almost always find themselves. In the excitement of discovery, as they begin to find new character, wholeness, and strength through service, they simply have no room for self-pity.

In the aftermath of a bloody battle during the Korean War, a war correspondent paused to watch a young Army nurse who was caring for some of the wounded. Standing over her shoulder, he leaned forward for a closer look just as she was removing the bandage from the leg of a badly injured soldier. He was caught off-guard by a glimpse of the gaping, oozing wound and the stench of blood and infection. He had to turn away to avoid becoming sick.

Thinking no one could hear him, the newsman muttered under his breath, "I wouldn't do that for a million bucks!"

"I wouldn't either," said the nurse, looking kindly up at him. "I do it for Jesus Christ."

Intrigued by her response, the correspondent began to talk with this nurse. He discovered she had lost her husband in an accident some months earlier. Her grief and loneliness seemed too much to bear. But during this time she made a choice to offer her nursing experience to God. This led her to service in Korea, just a few miles from the battlefront. "Once, all I cared about was financial security, a nice car, a nice house. Now I'm surrounded by all this blood, pain, and devastation—but I've never been more fulfilled. If I was home right now, I'd be clean and comfortable, but awash in self-pity. Here, my life has meaning." This nurse had learned one of the most important lessons in life: Christlike servanthood is the healing choice for the hurt of loneliness.

The great homesickness

I was twenty-one years old, hitchhiking across the beautiful Welsh countryside on a holiday from my studies at the University of London. My journey alternated between high exhilaration and deep loneliness. I sometimes reflected on all the miles that separated me from my family and friends in Iowa, and at times I even felt out of touch with God. Near the close of one day, feeling very homesick, I sat down on one of those green Welsh hillsides, shrugged off my backpack, and began to read from Psalm 139.

Where can I go from your Spirit?
Where can I flee from your presence?
If I go up to the heavens, you are there;
  If I make my bed in the depths, you are there.
If I rise on the wings of the dawn,
  If I settle on the far side of the sea,
Even there your hand will guide me,
  Your right hand will hold me fast.

As I was reading those words, I felt a quiet assurance wash over me: God Himself was with me. Though I was halfway around the world from home, He was beside me—and I no longer felt alone.

The human heart is afflicted with a longing, a homesickness that is so deep and so vast that only something very much larger than ourselves can fill it. "Loneliness is none other than homesickness for God," Lloyd Ogilvie once wrote. "Intimate communion with Him is our home."

All our human relationships, as important as they are, are *horizontal* relationships. Our relationship with God is of a different dimension: it is *vertical.* God reaches down to us in our loneliness and lifts us up toward communion with Him. The wonderful paradox God offers us is that in order to escape the prison of our loneliness, we must learn the discipline of *solitude.* We are homesick for God, and freedom from loneliness can only come as we become increasingly intimate with God. This is what Jesus was telling us by the example of His life, as He spent many hours—and even entire nights—alone in prayer.

Intimacy with God is our home, and no matter where we are, He is never far from us. When we have a vital love-relationship with Him, how can we possibly feel alone? God is far greater than all the longings of our hearts, and when we lose ourselves in the love and wonder of His presence, we have true freedom from loneliness.

5

Healing the Hurt of Failure

Be valiant in the attempt, yet not ashamed to fail.
—Samuel Johnson

The race is not to the swift,
nor the battle to the strong.
—Ecclesiastes 9:11 (KJV)

One day, not long ago, the parents of a college student received a letter from their daughter which went something like this:

Dear Mom and Dad,
Just thought I'd drop you a note to clue you in on my plans. I've fallen in love with a guy named Jim. He quit high school after the eleventh grade to get married. He's been divorced now for about a year. Jim and I have been going steady for two months and we plan to get married in the fall. Until then, I've decided to move into his apartment.

By the way, I think I might be pregnant. At any rate, I dropped out of school last week, although I'd really like to finish college at some time in the future.

This young woman's parents hastily turned to page two of their daughter's letter and read:

Mom and Dad, I just want you to know that everything I've written so far in this letter is *false*. Not a word of it is true. But Mom and Dad, it *is* true that I got a C– in French and I flunked math.

I just wanted to put things in their proper perspective.

How we need the proper perspective on the times of setback and failure that are inevitable throughout our lives.

Richard Haydn, a comedic character actor of the 1940s and '50s, was noted for his highly original interpretation of a poem by Edgar A. Guest, *It Couldn't Be Done.* Haydn— the perfect image of a fogeyish professor in black bow tie and pince-nez—would stand stiffly, with his hands behind his back, and stuffily recite:

> Somebody said that it couldn't be done,
>> But he with a chuckle replied
> That "maybe it couldn't," but he would be one
>> Who wouldn't say so till he'd tried.

> So he buckled right in with a trace of a grin
>> On his face. If he worried he hid it.
> He started to sing as he tackled the thing
>> That couldn't be done—

> *And he couldn't do it.*

Edgar A. Guest, of course, wrote about a man who "tackled the thing that couldn't be done, and he *did* it"—a poem about effort, a positive attitude, and *success.* Haydn turned it into a story of failure—though he *never* failed to draw laughs from audiences who identified with the man who "couldn't do it."

We all know what it is like to try and fail. The Bible acknowledges that all of us, despite our best efforts, will know the hurt of failure. Ecclesiastes 9:1 reminds us that the race is not always to the swift, nor the battle to the strong. Time and circumstances sometimes overwhelm our dreams. Yet, if we're honest with ourselves, we have to admit that failure is not nearly so much what happens to us, but what happens *within* us. We fail outwardly because we have been inwardly negligent or undisciplined.

Keys to success

Accomplishment is never an accident. It requires thought, diligent planning, effort, and strength of character. I believe the first key to success is goal-setting, which is simply the hard work of *thinking* our way through to a direction in life.

If you go to a successful person and ask him what his goals are for the next year or five years or ten years of his life, he can probably tell you without pausing to think. His goals are clearly before him all the time.

Say you want to see improvement in your physical fitness over the next several years: First, you can sit down and plan out where you want to be in terms of your weight, heart rate, and blood pressure at certain intervals in your life. Then you can decide what you will need to do to achieve those goals: a diet program, an exercise program, a schedule of checkups with your doctor.

You can develop a similar set of goals for all the areas of your life: professional and financial goals, educational or intellectual goals, and most importantly, spiritual goals. Our plans should not be rigid and inflexible, lest unforeseen circumstances derail and discourage us. But we need always to keep our goal before us, even if we have to take a few detours along the way; if we aim at nothing, then nothing is exactly what we are most likely to hit.

The second key to success is to set priorities. It's easy for most of us to allow the most "urgent" things to crowd out those things that are truly the most important. We can end up spending so much time "putting out fires" that we never get to accomplish the things we truly feel God is calling us to do. That means we're going to have to learn to say "No" to some good things so we can say "Yes" to the best things.

An example of the failure to set proper priorities would be the successful businessman who becomes the envy of his colleagues at the same time his family life is crumbling. He has been so ambitious in his career that he has neglected his family—and one day he awakes to realize that he has failed as a husband and father. Another example: the pastor or Christian layperson who diligently performs years of Christian service, only to discover that his faith has become hollow and the God he's tried to serve has now become a stranger to him; it's easy to allow our relationship with God to be squeezed out by Christian "busy-ness." Unless we periodically take time to sort out our priorities, we will never reach our most important goals.

The third key to success is to accept complete personal

responsibility for our problems and failures. In *The Road Less Traveled,* Dr. M. Scott Peck writes,

> We must accept responsibility for a problem before we can solve it. We cannot solve a problem by saying "It's not my problem." We cannot solve a problem by hoping that someone else will solve it for us. I can solve a problem only when I say, "This is *my* problem and it's up to me to solve it." But many, so many, seek to avoid the pain of their problems by saying to themselves, "This problem was caused me by other people, or by social circumstances beyond my control, and therefore it is up to other people or society to solve this problem for me. It is not really my personal problem." [1]

As long as our focus is on making excuses or shifting blame, we will continue to experience failure because we will fail to learn, to grow, and to change. But as we accept responsibility for our lives and make the healing choice to truly *learn* from our failures, then we can begin to transform the failed patterns of the past into new patterns of future success. This learning process can continue throughout our lives, turning our everyday existence into a lifelong *adventure.*

The pressure of failure

Shortly after I was ordained a pastor, I started a young people's singing group in our Minneapolis church. Called The Children of Hope, this group performed around the Midwest, sharing about Christ in song and testimony. Following one concert, I gave a ten-minute message, after which we greeted people in the back of the auditorium. One woman came up to me, put her hand on my arm, and said, "Young man, I see real potential in you. I think you could be a good speaker some day, maybe even a preacher! Now, what you need to do is to go on to college and take some speech courses, and then you should go on to seminary—"

"Excuse me, ma'am—" one of the boys in our group interrupted. "He's already been to college and seminary. You see, he's our preacher and—well, that's the best he can do!"

An example of one woman's good-intentioned attempt to give encouragement—an attempt which failed. On a more serious level, many of our failures are like that; the road to failure is paved with good intentions—and bad timing. Often we fail in the attempt to do God's will because we try to do it our own way. We see a need and we rush to meet that need without stopping to ask God for wisdom and discernment. So in our attempt to help we often hurt instead. We have good intentions, but we are not in God's timing.

Whether our failure is a great fiasco or a minor embarrassment, our deepest need is to discover God's perspective on our failure. Few of us have the kind of perspective on failure that J. B. Phillips had when he paraphrased James 1:2—"When all kinds of trials and failures crowd into your lives, my brothers, don't resent them as intruders, but welcome them as friends. Realize that they come to test your faith and produce in you the quality of endurance." As we work to gain this kind of perspective, we should be aware that there are two forms of *pressure* we will almost always feel in those inevitable times when we stumble and fail:

First, in times of failure we will feel *the pressure of our own guilt.* Most of us heap a load of self-reproach onto our honest mistakes—especially those of us with so-called "Type A" personalities. We are programmed with a success mentality, preoccupied with unrealistically high standards. Longfellow once wrote, "Most people would succeed in small things if they were not troubled with lofty ambitions." It's true: when we set unattainable goals for ourselves, we set ourselves up for failure.

I do it myself all the time—writing out such a long "Things to Do" list I can never get it all done in a day. But God is much more compassionate toward us than we are toward ourselves. As the psalmist wrote, "He knows our frame." He never sets unrealistic standards for us. It's taken me a long time to learn this lesson: God doesn't want our activity; He wants our maturity. He wants our *will* more than He wants our *works.*

Secondly, in times of failure we will feel *the pressure of people.* Too often, our favorite indoor sport, even as Christians, is to kick the one who is down. But when you've failed, you already know it; you don't need someone to say, "You blew it." You need someone in your corner, someone to build you up again.

In Lorraine Hansberry's play *A Raisin in the Sun,* there is a poignant depiction of failure. The father of a poor inner-city black family has just died, leaving only a small life-insurance policy. His widow has a dream of using this money to buy a small bungalow in a better part of town. Her son, however, wants to invest the money in a business deal, which he believes can multiply the small legacy. This young man, who has never held a job, sincerely wants to do something to help his family. He pleads with his mother for the money; she refuses at first, but finally relents and gives her son most of the money. He then invests it with a "friend"—and this "friend" skips town with the cash.

When the young man confesses his failure to his mother and sister, the sister flies into a rage, cursing him and condemning him for being so stupid, for gambling away their future. But suddenly the mother steps in, cutting off the sister's tirade. "I thought I taught you to love your brother," she says.

"Love him?" shouts the sister. "There's nothing left to love!"

"There's *always* something left to love—and if you ain't learned that, you ain't learned nothing!" the mother replies. "Have you cried for that boy today? Not for yourself because that money's gone, but for *him,* for what he's been through! Child, when do you think is the time to love somebody the most? When he's done good? That ain't the time at all. It's when he's at his lowest and can't believe in himself 'cause the world done whipped him so!" [2]

That's what God's unconditional love is like in our times of failure. God is always there in your corner, and He wants to get you back into action, not count you out. People may accuse you or write you off after you've failed—but not God.

There's a saying, "You can't knock success." At the same time, I submit that there's something to be said for failure. I don't think I'm being at all glib about this; I honestly believe that some of the greatest growth in my life has come in the aftermath of my biggest mistakes. This is especially true of those times I've failed miserably, and there have been people in my life who have continued to love me and affirm me through it all.

A well-known Christian spokesman made a claim in a recent television commercial that the Bible says, " 'In everything you

do, put God first, and He will direct you and crown your
efforts with success.' " The passage quoted in this commercial
is Proverbs 3:6, as rendered by a popular paraphrased version
of the Bible. At first glance, it might seem that God is saying,
"I'll make you a deal: Put me first in all you do—and I'll
make you successful!"

But is this what the Bible really says? Both the *New International Version* and the *New American Standard Bible* translate
this verse, "In all your ways acknowledge him, and he will
make your paths straight." Clearly, Proverbs 3:6 is God's
promise to guide us in the paths *He* chooses. This is a great
promise—but it's not a promise that we will never fail! The
path He chooses for us may lead us through the trial of failure.
We need to learn that failure is not such an awful tragedy.
The *real* tragedy is when we go through failure and learn
nothing from it.

As Paul wrote in 1 Corinthians 1:27, "God chose the foolish
things of the world to shame the wise; God chose the weak
things of the world to shame the strong." And if we are honest,
we have to confess that God sometimes chooses the seeming
failures of this world to shame the apparent successes of this
world. God's guarantee to us is not that He will crown our
efforts with success, but that we are permitted to fail.

Your response: your responsibility

One of my favorite places to turn to when I'm experiencing
the hurt of failure is Psalm 103. There, in verses 1 and 2,
David writes, "Praise the Lord, O my soul; all my inmost
being, praise his holy name. Praise the Lord, O my soul, and
forget not all his benefits." In this Psalm, David is speaking
to his inner self, his soul, as if to say, "Be grateful to God!
Even though I'm hurting now, I refuse to focus on my failure.
Instead, I choose to focus on gratefully remembering all the
blessings God has brought into my life!"

My friend Elton "Gil" Gillam, founder of Church Prayer
Ministry International, raises a question that I find helpful,
and even crucial, as I try to respond to the hurt of failure in
my own life. He asks, "Are you gazing or just glancing at
God?" Whenever we find ourselves facing problems, our human tendency is to gaze at our circumstances while merely

glancing at God. Our perspective is reversed, as if we were looking through the wrong end of the telescope: our problems loom large while God appears small. We need to learn to keep our gaze on God while glancing at our circumstances.

Even when life has flattened our dreams with a steamroller, we can still make the healing choice to remember God's benefits, to seek His face, to keep our gaze on Him. No matter how bad our circumstances, our response is our responsibility. If we keep our gaze on God, we can get up and keep advancing toward our goal. But if we gaze at our circumstances, we'll lose sight of our goal, and sink into a mire of self-pity.

What are the benefits of God that we are to recall in our trial of failure? David names some of them in Psalm 103:3: "He forgives all [your] sins." *All.* Even the sins that brought us down into failure? Yes, even those. Sin and failure are not the end of the line for us. God calls us to repent and be forgiven, and His grace is always there. God's grace means nothing less than a completely fresh start.

Another benefit is listed for us in Psalm 103:10—"He does not treat us as our sins deserve or repay us according to our iniquities." God's love for us is unconditional. He doesn't say, "If you succeed, then I'll accept you and love you. If you don't fail Me, then you'll win My favor." God accepts us and loves us right where we are.

We should take our cue from God in our relationships with each other. What a tragedy that we put so many pressures on people to think the way we think, to succeed on our terms and never fail us, before we will say, "I love you, I accept you." The distinction between God's love and the love of this world is precisely this: God's love is unconditional.

A surgeon wrote these words shortly after performing surgery on the face of a pretty young woman:

> I stand by the bed where a young woman lies, her face postoperative, her mouth twisted in palsy. A tiny twig of the facial nerve, the one to the muscles of her mouth, has been severed. She will be thus from now on. . . . To remove the tumor in her cheek, I had to cut the little nerve.
> Her young husband is in the room. He stands on the opposite side of the bed, and together they seem to dwell in the evening lamplight, isolated from me, private. . . .

"Will my mouth always be like this?" she asks.
"Yes," I say, "it will. It's because the nerve was cut."
"I like it," he says. "It's kind of cute." . . . Unmindful,
he bends to kiss her crooked mouth, and I so close I
can see how he twists his own lips to accommodate hers,
to show her that their kiss still works.[3]

That's what God's love is like. He reaches out to the deformities
and failures we have made of our lives, and He gives us a
cue as to how we are to relate to one another. God is the
One to whom we can turn—even in the worst of our failures—
to receive His amazing touch of grace and forgiveness.

David describes this kind of unconditional love in Psalm
103:11–12, "For as high as the heavens are above the earth,
so great is his love for those who fear him; as far as the east
is from the west, so far has he removed our transgressions
from us." He remembers our sins and failures no more; they're
buried in the deepest sea. Some of us have carried a weight
of guilt and self-reproach for years. God wants to free us from
that weight, and give us His freely flowing grace and forgiveness. Our focus when failure comes should be on grace, not
guilt.

Failure is *never* the end. It certainly wasn't the end for
Peter. This bold, self-confident disciple was so sure, so determined to stand by Jesus no matter what came; but when Jesus
was led away to be crucified, Peter's courage and determination
failed. He not only forsook his friend Jesus, but before the
night was over he had actually denied Him, and sealed his
denials with a terrible oath.

Peter was a miserable failure, and he knew it. But failure
wasn't the end of Peter's story. John 21 records that, following
the Resurrection, Jesus met Peter by the Sea of Galilee. There
He mercifully forgave and restored Peter, charging him with
an awesome responsibility: "Feed my sheep," shepherd the
new community which was to become the Church. Writing
in *Discipleship Journal,* Stephen D. Shores finds application
for our own trial of failure in the story of Peter:

> Could God forgive such a colossal failure? Was Peter
> even worth the try? Are we? Yes! . . . Peter found himself
> not only forgiven but trusted. He learned that failure is
> not the ultimate.

Failure is the unforgivable sin in American culture—so much so that it often paralyzes the individual in a deep-freeze of depression, self-condemnation, and resignation. The Bible, though, is full of the idea that our failures are not irreversible in their effects. Peter failed utterly but not ultimately, for God used him as an awesome force in the early Church. Our Father's ability to forgive and restore far outweighs our capacity for failure.[4]

Failure was not the end of the line for Peter. It was a *lesson*—and a new beginning. So it is with you and me. We can grow through failure, we can be changed by it so we can face even greater challenges in the future. Someone once said, "There is the greatest practical benefit in making a few failures early in life." Why? Because failure is not the end; it's the beginning of a new adventure.

A fresh start

An experience of failure often affects our sense of security. We begin to feel if we're not achieving, then perhaps we're not fully accepted by God. But God wants us to know that our true security lies not in our achievements, but in His unconditional love for us. Psalm 103:13–14 assures us, "As a father has compassion on his children, so the Lord has compassion on those who fear him; for he knows how we are formed, he remembers that we are dust." God accepts us as we are.

If God expects achievement from us before He will love us, then a friend of mine, Peggy, has nothing to look forward to. She is retarded, paralyzed from the neck down, and her capacity to achieve is severely limited. But I'm convinced Peggy receives abundant grace and love from God—not because she is accomplishing great things for Him, but because He accepts her unconditionally. He knows her heart.

And He knows your heart. When you fail, even when you fall flat on your face in full view of the whole world, God loves you just the same.

I confess I've lived most of my life from this false premise: "If I only achieve, people will love me more, God will love me more, and I'll be able to accept myself." Living that way is an emotional rollercoaster. Succeed at something and you're riding high—but just one moment of failure is all it takes to send your self-esteem plunging to the depths. God doesn't call us to that kind of life. He loves us even in our failure, and He wants us to see and accept ourselves just as He does.

The hurt of failure often leads us to compare ourselves with other people. We think, "I've worked harder and I'm more qualified than this other person, yet I've lost my job and he's getting a promotion!"

Or, "I've been a Christian longer than this other person in this church, yet his ministry is flourishing and mine is declining!"

Or, "We have a deeper relationship with Christ than those people, yet their children are Christians while our children have rebelled against God!"

Don't look at another person and say, "Compared to him or her, I'm a failure." If you compare your momentary failure with the momentary success of another person, you will probably end up in a prolonged depression. But if you compare your present failure with the everlasting love of God, a love that just goes on forever, you won't stay down for long.

Jesus always saw men and women not for what they *were,* but for what they were to *become.* That's the basis on which He chose the Twelve—seemingly a bunch of illiterates, malcontents, and selfish, petty failures. He knew what they would become, and so He allowed a lot of room for failure in their lives. He knew how they could learn and grow through failure. We need to learn that too.

A major failure is a sign that we need to make a significant change in life. It's time to relinquish the past and look to the future for a *new* challenge. Most of us can't keep from looking back, even when it's clear that the past is dead: "If only I could get my job back." Or, "If only I had my marriage again." Or, "If only I could change the fact of this bankruptcy." But we can't. The past is over; it's time for a fresh start.

Jesus: our example in failure

Isaiah 53:2 gives us a compelling portrait of a failure. His name: Jesus Christ. This messianic passage from the Old Testament says, "He had no beauty or majesty to attract us to him, nothing in his appearance that we should desire him."

In short, He looked like a failure. Where were His achievements and honors? What accomplishments was He recognized for?

He was born in the middle of nowhere to an unwed teenage girl. A mere three years of public ministry was all He could muster before He was hauled off and executed like a criminal. He was surrounded by illiterates and rabblerousers—and when He ended up on a cross, they deserted Him and left Him to die. His cause appeared lost. Men looked at Him and said, "How could this failure save anybody?"

Yet as Jesus offered Himself for our sin, He did nothing less than conquer sin and disarm death. He ascended from that tomb and *exploded* in resurrection power. This same Man who looked like such a failure to the world became the Redeemer of the world. It was Peter Marshall who said, "It is better to fail in a cause that will ultimately succeed than to succeed in a cause that will ultimately fail." Jesus knew that and He proved it.

Jesus is our example in failure. We may suffer setbacks and appear as fools before a scoffing world. But we know that our cause will ultimately succeed because the same Power that raised Jesus from the grave is working out His eternal plan through us.

There is an apocryphal story about a young man named Philo. According to the story, Philo was the only son of Pontius Pilate, the Roman official who ordered Christ's crucifixion. Even before Philo was born, Pilate had great ambitions for him. Pilate wanted a son who would one day be a great military leader, a son who would make him proud. But when Philo was born, Pilate's pride was dashed: Philo was born sick, weak, and permanently crippled. Throughout the years Philo was growing up, he was the object of his father's hatred and bitterness. "You're not the son I wanted," was Pilate's constant reminder to his broken son.

As soon as he was old enough to leave home, Philo left the palace of his father and wandered alone in the countryside. There he heard of a Galilean who went about preaching love, healing the sick and lame, and feeding the hungry. Philo sought out Jesus and Jesus healed him, not only physically but spiritually and emotionally. Philo was even able to forgive his father for making him feel like a failure as a son for all those years.

From then on, Philo followed Jesus wherever He went, and

it is said that on the day God's only Son Jesus was crucified, Pilate's only son Philo was at the foot of the cross, weeping over the death of his Lord and Friend.

Jesus has come to heal us of our deformities, to heal the past and point us toward the future. The sacrifice of Christ covers our sins and reconciles us to God—and He is sovereign over everything, including our failures. As we continue to gain more and more of God's perspective on the sins and mistakes of the past, we will increasingly see that failure is never the end, but a truly new beginning.

6

Healing the Hurt
of Inferiority

*To accept yourself positively and live creatively . . .
is the way to joy, but to deny and reject God's gift
of yourself is the way to ruin.*

—John Claypool

*You are a chosen people, a royal priesthood, a holy
nation, a people belonging to God, that you may
declare the praises of him who called you out of
darkness into his wonderful light.*

—1 Peter 2:9

As usual, he closed the front door behind himself and wearily announced, "I'm home!" He set down his briefcase and newspaper by his easy chair and began to loosen his tie, muttering, "What a day. . . ." Pressures, problems, and forty-five minutes' overtime!

"Dinner'll be ready in fifteen minutes, dear!" came a lilting voice from the kitchen.

"Thanks, sweetheart!" he replied. He sank into his easy chair, sighed deeply, and opened the newspaper. He only got as far as the first headline when—

"Daddy! Play football with me!" The four-year-old halfback scampered into his father's lap, fumbled his Nerf football, and sent sections of the *Chronicle* fluttering out of his father's hands.

"Ooof!" said Daddy, snatching at the newspaper which slithered, section by section, onto the floor. "Oh, son, I'm too tired to—" Then something in the newspaper caught his eye: a full-page advertisement featuring a NASA photograph of the earth. Inspired, he started tearing the ad in pieces.

"Son, I'm going to make a puzzle out of this picture of the world. Now I want you to put the world back together, okay?" He handed the pieces to his boy, then settled back for what he thought would be *at least* fifteen minutes of uninterrupted reading.

His boy was gone for just a little less than two minutes. "See!" he announced, proudly holding the picture of the earth, completely reassembled and held together with shiny Scotch tape.

The father blinked. "How did you do that so *fast*?!"

"It was easy!" said the boy. He turned the newspaper puzzle over, which revealed a picture of a man. "I just put the man together. And when I did that, the world came together, too!"

The world is a broken place, filled with broken people. But the gospel of Jesus Christ is the good news of wholeness for a broken world. The world can never be mended until we begin the task of mending our broken selves.

"In my judgment," says John Claypool, "there is no issue of any greater practical significance than the issue of self-image." As I consider all the people with whom I've counseled and prayed, I can think of no more universal human problem than that of broken self-image and feelings of inferiority. I'm convinced that *all* of us, to some degree, know the hurt of feeling inferior, feeling broken in our sense of self-worth. Some of us experience deep, unrelenting pain because the puzzle of our personality lies in pieces, and we feel no hope of *ever* reassembling the picture of ourselves as people of worth and value.

Feelings of inferiority almost always seem to begin in childhood. Self-image problems usually occur as parents compare their children according to a false scale of values which have been determined by the culture. The two most deceptive values on this scale, according to Christian psychologist Dr. James Dobson, are what he calls "Beauty: The Gold Coin of Human Worth," and "Intelligence: The Silver Coin of Human Worth." In his book *Hide or Seek,* Dobson observes that a common tragedy of childhood is that so many parents expect their children to be, first, beautiful, and second, smart—and when they don't quite measure up to these standards, feelings of inferiority usually set in.[1]

Other children sometimes join in the process of breaking down self-esteem with cruel teasing or isolation of a child. Then comes adolescence, with its tentative first contacts between the sexes, its rapid physical transformations, and its Clearasil crises—a time of life when most young people begin to feel too short, too tall, too fat, too skinny, too awkward, too shy, too much something, or not enough something else. Many of us have experienced the brutal assassination of our self-image by our peers when we were at a vulnerable stage in life. The hurt of old wounds can stab as deeply as if it were only yesterday.

In adulthood, we find ourselves barraged by an endless stream of films, songs, magazines, televisions shows, and commercials—all *calculated* to make us feel inferior. This planned assault on our self-esteem is designed to motivate us to buy a range of wonder-products which will magically rid us of our inferiority feelings. So it's no wonder we grow up feeling short-changed in the coinage of human worth, that we see ourselves as unlovely and unloved.

The Red Queen's Race

We act out our inferiority feelings in various ways. Some withdraw into a shell of painful shyness. Others mask their inner hurt, compensating for a sense of inferiority by assuming an air of *superiority.* That conceited, self-important person you find so unbearable is probably trying to prove to himself that he's not really as insignificant and inferior as he unconsciously feels he is.

Others respond to inferiority feelings by desperately seeking the acceptance of others. Some, in fact, become so intent on gaining approval and meeting the expectations of others that they never authentically become *themselves.* I've been down that road, and I found that hiding my true self to avoid being rejected never ended my sense of inadequacy; it only compounded my problems.

Tucked away in a quiet corner of Scripture, there's a phrase that brims with emotion, ancient words from the pen of Job: "The souls of the wounded cry out" (Job 24:12). Maybe your soul is crying out even now; I've felt that way many times. All of us have been wounded in our self-image at one time or another, and whether we tend to respond to these wounds with shyness, or a mask of superiority, or by seeking approval, there is a healing choice we can make for the hurt of inferiority.

How do we begin building a stronger self-image into ourselves and those we love?

We can learn a lot from the example of a man named Fred Rogers. If you have small children, you probably already know the host of Public Broadcasting's *Mister Rogers' Neighborhood.* In 1963, Mr. Rogers was ordained a Presbyterian minister with the special charge to "serve children and their families through the media," and he's been lovingly ministering to children on public TV ever since.

There's no secret to building self-esteem. As Mr. Rogers has demonstrated every weekday for the past twenty years, it's something a child can understand. He sings songs that tell children, "You are my friend, you are special to me," and "I like you just the way you are." He helps children to believe in themselves, to be kind to one another, and to understand that everybody is wonderfully unique.

Mr. Rogers knows the difference between *affirming* someone and *flattering* someone. Flattery doesn't build self-esteem; it only reinforces a pattern of approval-seeking. Flattery says, "I love you *because* you do the things that win my acceptance." Embedded in such statements is the tacit (and frightening) condition: "And I will love you *only* so long as you continue to please me."

Authentic affirmation, however, builds security and healthy self-worth. Affirmation says, "You don't have to earn my acceptance. I love you just the way you are. I'll never pressure you to be anyone but who you are. I'll always love you, and nothing you will ever do can change that."

In the classic children's fantasy *Through the Looking Glass,* Lewis Carroll pictures a scene in which little Alice is running hand-in-hand with a chess-piece, the Red Queen. Though Alice runs as fast as she can, trying to keep up, the Queen repeatedly shouts, "Faster! Faster!" But as fast as they run, the scenery never changes.

Finally, Alice and the Queen collapse under a tree—the same tree from which they started. "Why, we've gotten absolutely nowhere!" gasps Alice. "Everything's just as it was!"

"Of course!" sniffs the Queen. "In the Red Queen's Race, it takes all the running you can do just to keep in the same place! If you want to get somewhere else, you must run twice as fast as that!"

The Red Queen's Race is a dead-heat on a treadmill, with the finish line forever beyond reach. The race for acceptance so many of us run is the Red Queen's Race of the Soul: our goal—secure self-worth—is always in sight, but never in reach. The finish line is a mirage. There's no way to win, no way to get off. In the Red Queen's Race, self-esteem rises and falls on the see-saw of achievement and failure.

Lauren Tewes was sprinting in the fast lane of the Red Queen's Race. A recent *TV Guide* cover story relates that she was making more than a million dollars a year as the co-star of a top-rated television series.[2] Talent, beauty, and personality combined to make her one of the most recognized people in the world. But despite the glamor that surrounded her public image, her private life became a struggle for self-worth from her first days on the set. Studio executives criticized her mercilessly. "I felt so insecure," she said. "I spent a lot of time trying to please people who demanded I change myself. They told me I was a star, but I felt like nothing."

In the attempt to escape her prison of insecurity, she sought refuge in the euphoria of cocaine. But this drug eventually stole everything from her, including the last remaining tatters of her self-esteem. She was fired from the series and forced to begin a long, slow struggle to rebuild her career from scratch. Only seven years after she attained television stardom, her career, her money, and her home were gone—traded for cocaine.

One morning after a sleepless night, feeling worthless and totally alone, she turned on the television and fell into bed. The screen flickered to life, and a kindly man in a red cardigan sweater smiled and said, "I'll be your friend. Will you be mine?"

The young actress broke down in tears and answered him aloud, "Yes."

"I resolved at that point to get my life together," she later said. "I was totally collapsed, and Mr. Rogers saved my life." On that day, she began the long process of withdrawing from cocaine and rebuilding her career—and the one who gave her the courage to believe in herself was Fred Rogers. With just a few simple words of friendship in a children's television show, he had helped to change the direction of this young woman's life. Rumor has it that Lauren will be reinstated as cruise director of the "Love Boat" this fall. You never know when

a quiet, simple act—a hug, a smile, or a word of friendship—
might rescue someone from despair.

Worm theology

Jesus taught, "Blessed are the poor in spirit." The apostle
Paul wrote, "I know that nothing good lives in me." Martin
Luther said, "God creates out of nothing, and until a man
becomes nothing, God can make nothing out of him." And
Christianity has long been misunderstood on this point. Many
people have historically seen Christianity as teaching the *aboli-
tion* of human self-worth.

In response, a secular movement has arisen, saying, "Look
out for Number One! Be your own best friend! Be good to
yourself! You're *worth* it!" Best-selling books, TV talk shows,
and advertising have joined forces to proclaim, "You can have
self-esteem—and we'll sell it to you!" So the church, afraid
of losing its audience, has chimed in, "Oh, yes! We believe
that too!" and desperately tried to tack the name of Jesus
onto the secular self-fulfillment fad.

The problem is that society's approach to realizing self-
worth stands opposed to the authentic sense of worth found
in Scripture. These two approaches cannot be synthesized.
Whereas the self-fulfillment movement says, "Find self-worth
through achievement and self-sufficiency," the Bible says, in
effect, "Self-esteem lies in how we are unconditionally loved
and valued by God."

Isaac Watts wrote over six hundred hymns, and probably
the best-loved of all those hymns is the one which contains
the words:

> Alas! and did my Savior bleed,
> And did my Sovereign die?
> Would He devote that sacred Head
> For such a worm as I?

As much as I love that hymn, I'm troubled by that last phrase.
I wonder what it does to our image of ourselves to ask, "Why
should Christ have gone to the Cross for a *worm* like me?"
Certainly, as we look back on our lives, we can't escape the
conclusion that we stand flawed and sinful before God. Clearly,

this is the truth Watts intended to portray in this hymn. The trouble is many of us grew up in homes and churches where "worm theology" is all we ever heard.

If Jesus Christ is the Savior and Lord of your life, then it's time to shed your "worm theology" and begin seeing yourself as God sees you. The Bible says that you are fearfully and wonderfully made, created in the image of God. As a follower of Christ, you have been chosen and endowed with special gifts to fill a unique place in the church. You are a child of His handiwork, a saint, part of a royal priesthood, a joint-heir with Christ.

Chuck Swindoll once said, "No one who actually hates himself can adequately share the love of Christ." Why? Because Jesus taught us to love others *as we love ourselves.* When we are hindered in our ability to unconditionally accept ourselves, we are crippled in our capacity to effectively love others.

Not long ago, I was talking to a young man whose life is beginning to reflect a healthy sense of self-esteem and Christian dignity. That was not always the case. He had grown up in a number of churches, beginning with a Roman Catholic church until he was nine years old, followed by two mainline Protestant churches, a fundamentalist church, and a charismatic fellowship. "In every one of those churches," he told me, "I heard dignity and self-esteem condemned. I was made to feel doomed as a sinner unless I condemned myself—so I did. I actually began to *hate* myself."

But he brightened as he said, "Then I had a new encounter with Christ. And He didn't tell me how bad I was—I already knew that. He just told me how great I was going to become as we walked on through life together!" This young man had discovered the liberating truth of the gospel: Jesus has come to set us free from our feelings of inferiority. He didn't die for worms, but for men and women made in the image of God.

A grand performance—or an act of love?

The composer Verdi stood in the shadows of the concert hall in Florence during the performance of his very first opera. Though he would later garner the acclaim of the music world, at this point in his career he was unknown. Throughout the performance Verdi waited in the darkness with his eye on one person in the audience: the master composer Rossini. Verdi did not care whether the crowd would cheer him or jeer him. All he wanted was the smile of approval from the master.

Most of us tend to be very fragile, sensitive to the least slight or slur. That's because we seek approval from the world; we let others determine our opinion of ourselves. But when our object is to please the Master alone, then even the most cruel slap of rejection cannot harm our inner being; we become invincible. As a wise friend once told me, "I'm gradually learning to play out my life before a grand audience of One." It's a lesson I'm gradually learning, too.

I have to confess that I'm crippled. I don't wear braces on my arms or legs, but I'm crippled spiritually and emotionally. The Great Physician is bringing healing to my crippled self-image, but even as I write these words, I'm still inching my way toward wholeness.

For much of my life I sought the recognition of my peers. I can see clearly now that I really wanted that approval more than I wanted God. My sense of inadequacy grew worse as I entered high school and college. I was sprinting full-tilt on that treadmill race for self-acceptance, and the finish line was always beyond my reach.

Then, as a freshman in college, I met Jesus Christ in a dramatic way. I had been raised in a Christian home, and had grown up with a faith in Christ as Savior, but on this particular occasion I met Him as *Lord*. That's when a great *tension* moved into my life—tension between my desire to serve Jesus Christ and that deeply ingrained drive to be accepted for my achievements.

In my new commitment to Christ, I felt like a reborn person, with a newfound enthusiasm for boldly sharing Christ with others. Yet around my closest friends—whose approval I desperately wanted—I remained silent about my new relationship with Christ, afraid to be labeled a "religious fanatic." There was a tension between pleasing Christ and pleasing others.

Soon after giving my life to Christ, I felt the call of God to preach the gospel. At the age of eighteen, I began preaching in small churches, youth rallies, and meetings. But even as I preached, I knew there was a duality in my personality—the tension between wanting to preach Christ and wanting to gain some recognition and praise for myself.

Then, about ten years ago, I accepted an invitation to give the commencement address at the seminary from which I had graduated some years earlier. As I went, I knew I was going with tainted motives. I wanted to preach Christ—but I also hungered for recognition. I got no sleep at all the night before I was to speak.

The next day on the platform, as I awaited my turn to speak, I was filled with anxiety. My hands shook so badly I could hardly read my notes. I prayed that God would give me His peace, but no peace came. Then some words came to me through my conscience, just as though God were saying, "Ron, the reason you're so nervous is that you want to impress people. I don't need you to impress these people. I need you to love them. Ron, I don't need a Grand Performance. I want your life to be an Act of Love."

That was a transforming moment for me. My inner obsession with obtaining praise and honor fell away like a weight. The message I shared that day was not much different from what I had planned to say, but the heart from which it flowed was beginning to be changed.

Yet my struggle is not ended. The apostle Paul, writing in Galatians 1:10, delves unerringly into my own crisis of self-acceptance with this question: "Am I now trying to win the approval of men, or of God? Am I trying to please men? If I were still trying to please men, I would not be a servant of Christ." This is probably the most convicting portion of Scripture in all my life and ministry. I wrestle with the truth of Galatians 1:10 literally every day.

Today, virtually every time I get up to speak, I hear the words come back to my mind, "Not a Grand Performance, but an Act of Love." I've lived most of my life for the sake of impressing others, and a lifelong pattern does not change overnight. I'm still involved in a process of becoming healed of the hurt of inferiority.

We're all crippled. We all have feelings of inadequacy in our lives, and these feelings hold us back from being everything God wants us to be. God never intended us to feel beaten down by the past or paralyzed by a sense of inferiority. Rather, He calls us to make the healing choice for the hurt of inferiority—the choice to dwell on His *truth* about ourselves:

We are made in God's image, chosen to be His children. He bought us with the blood of His Son Jesus because we are incalculably precious in His eyes. We are men and women of value and importance, children of light in a dying age. *These are the truths that heal us of the hurt of inferiority—truths which give our lives meaning in the eternal plan of God.*

7

Healing the Hurt of Doubt

In order to believe greatly, one must doubt greatly.
—Malcolm Muggeridge

Now we see but a poor reflection; then we shall see face to face. Now I know in part; then I shall know fully, even as I am fully known.
—1 Corinthians 13:12

Not long ago, I received a letter from my friend Tom. The last time I had seen him, he was an active lay leader in a church in the Midwest. "The process of the erosion of my faith has taken years," he now wrote, "but now it's entirely gone. I feel like my life is ended. A few years ago, I was a strong Christian with what I thought was an invincible faith. Now I'm just a hollow shell. I feel so unworthy in my church because of my doubts."

To many of us, doubt is the deep, dark secret of the Christian life, a skeleton in the closet of almost every Christian's soul. Most of us are afraid to confess our doubts and questions because we're afraid others will judge us for our doubts, or perhaps because we're afraid our doubts might "rub off" on others and hinder their faith. And since everyone else is just like us, afraid to be honest about their doubts, we usually feel very much alone with our most troubling questions.

Perhaps you've had an experience like this: A question about your faith has been gnawing at you. You try to put it out of your mind, but it keeps coming back to haunt you. You feel you're the only person in the world who has been plagued with this particular doubt. One evening, you're in a Bible study, or having coffee with some Christian friends, and you venture to open up a little and confess your doubt to those friends—

Usually one of two things will happen. Your friends may gasp and begin to reprimand you. They may tell you it's a sin to doubt. In short, they may cause you to feel *unworthy* because of your doubts. That's what happened to my friend Tom. "I feel so unworthy in my church," he wrote, "because of my doubts." Sometimes our Christian friends have a hard time accepting the honest struggle of faith we go through.

However, you may get a different response when you confess your doubts. You may hear one of your friends say, "I know what you mean. I've felt that way, too." And another friend may say, "You have doubts like that too? I thought I was the only one!" And another, "I really appreciate your openness. It really helps me to hear that the doubts I've been feeling aren't so unusual."

We need to see doubting not as the enemy, but as a necessary component of faith. I can affirm the words of Alfred Lord Tennyson, "There lives more faith in honest doubt, believe me, than in half the creeds." This doesn't mean that doctrines are unimportant, but rather that courageously testing the reality of our faith has more meaning than the rote-reciting of some doctrinal statement. Doubts are an inevitable part of life and faith. When times of doubt come we should face our questions, not run from them.

I've seen it again and again: broken faith, like broken bones, almost always mends stronger than before.

Jesus and the doubter

The Bible affirms that there is room for questioning in our pilgrimage toward mature Christian faith. We need to have the same reverent skepticism we see in the Bereans of Acts 17:11, who "examined the Scriptures every day to see if what Paul said was true." As A. W. Tozer wrote, "We would do well to cultivate a reverent skepticism. . . . It is no sin to doubt some things, but it may be fatal to believe everything." [1] Tozer's words are prophetic indeed: if only there had been more doubters in Jonestown, Guyana! Indeed, the many cults that proliferate today could not long exist if they permitted this kind of reverent doubting.

Jesus gave us the right to inquire into truth when He proclaimed Himself to be the Way, the Truth, and the Life. In John 8:31–32, He told those who had chosen to believe Him, "If you hold to my teaching, you are really my disciples. Then you will know the truth, and the truth will set you free." Certainly, it takes belief, it takes *holding* to Jesus' teaching to really be His disciple. But Jesus also promised that we will know the truth, and the truth will set us free. Thus Jesus sanctifies the human process of rational inquiry, and He honors the human intellect, which was fashioned by the intellect of God.

Many of us have never noticed in the Scriptures how tenderly Jesus dealt with the doubters whose lives He touched. Remember John the Baptist, languishing alone in prison, awaiting his death? He had once proclaimed Jesus to crowds of people, but now he had begun to doubt. So he sent messengers to Jesus, asking, "Are you the One who was to come—or should we expect someone else?" Jesus sent those messengers back to John with His assurances, then turned to those around Him and affirmed John, even in the midst of his doubts: "I tell you, among those born of women, there is no one greater than John."

Remember Peter, who despaired so deeply in his faith that he actually denied Christ three times? Jesus' gentle response to Peter was to affirm him, to reinstate him in his faith, to tell him, "Go, Peter, and feed my sheep."

And remember Thomas, that classic I'm-from-Missouri skeptic who adamantly refused to believe the report of his friends that Jesus had been raised from the dead? "Unless I see the nail marks in his hands and put my finger where the nails were, and put my hand into his side," he declared, "I will not believe it!" You can almost feel the warmth of Jesus' smile and the tenderness in His voice when He appeared to Thomas and said, "Put your fingers here, Thomas. See my hands. Reach out your hand and put it into my side." Jesus did not rebuke Thomas for his doubts; rather, He invited Thomas's inquiry into the truth of the Resurrection.

Doubt is a valid part of our pilgrimage of faith, too. As we ponder our honest questions about our faith, Jesus would deal just as gently and affirmingly with us as He did with John the Baptist, Peter, and Thomas. God has given us the ability to reason, to wonder, to question—and He wants to use our intellect to bring us to an authentic faith in Him. T. M. Kitwood writes that the denial of honest questioning in our faith amounts to "the crucifixion of the intellect." He explains,

> This means that the believer, never being convinced in his mind, cannot give the full assent of his personality to God. He cannot believe with integrity. This is a serious departure from the Christianity of Christ who, though proclaiming . . . a revelation of God's truth, constantly appealed to the mind and the critical faculty.[2]

God calls us to a truly realistic and biblical kind of faith which touches us in our totality. Our faith will be a sound and reliable anchor for our lives only when it deeply involves *all* parts of our humanity, including our intellect.

Faith doesn't have to be blind

All around us, our fellow Christians are struggling with deep and troubling questions of their faith. Are we helping them work through their doubts? Jude verse 22 tells us, "Be merciful to those who doubt." Not critical, not easily shocked, not judgmental, but *merciful.*

The evangelical church has been slow to acknowledge the role of doubt in faith. In some ways, the church has been buying into the growing antirational, anti-intellectual mood of the dying culture in which we live—the mood that says there is no certainty, no objective truth in life; there is only a choice between "blind faith" or despair. It's time we affirm that blindness in one's faith is a handicap, just as physical blindness is a handicap in the physical world.

Many parents today are blindfolding their children intellectually, and thereby handicapping their faith even as they seek to protect them from error. I have two children, and I love them so much that I would spare them the hurt of doubt in any way I could. Yet to do so would actually hurt them in the long run because they *need* these growing pains of faith to become strong mentally, emotionally, and spiritually.

Those parents who desperately try to shield their children

from doubts are leaving them defenseless. It won't be long before an agnostic friend or teacher poses some hard questions to them—questions they can't answer, questions they were never allowed to think about before. Francis Schaeffer once said that of all the troubled young people who journeyed to his L'Abri retreat in Switzerland—bringing their deep confusion and anxiety about their faith—the vast majority came not from nonbelieving homes, but from evangelical or fundamentalist homes which communicated to them, "Don't question, just believe!"

It's normal and healthy for children, as they go through adolescence, to begin to question the values they've received from their parents. As children begin to approach adulthood, they naturally begin to establish their own separate identity. They need to come to a place where the Christian faith is authentically *their* faith, not just something handed down to them. When our young people doubt, it doesn't mean they're going to reject the Christian faith. It simply means they will ask questions—and we need to help them find the answers. We will never strengthen their faith by denying their questions.

Tragically, many parents feel threatened by the doubts and questions of their children. They react strongly—and their children are repelled rather than convinced. When our children come to us with their honest doubts, we have an opportunity to welcome and affirm their hunger for knowledge. We can respect their God-given intellect and say, "I'm glad you asked. That's a hard question, and I've wondered about it myself. Maybe we could try to find the answer together." And then we can seek out a relevant book or Scripture passage or a knowledgeable person for help and insight.

When our children have learned not to be afraid of the truth, but to *embrace* the truth, they will have a strong foundation for a living, growing faith. If the gospel doesn't make sense amid doubts and intellectual questioning, then it doesn't make sense at all. But thank God, the gospel does make sense. Our faith doesn't have to be "blind faith."

Doubting in the darkness

Our hardest trials of doubt come as an accompaniment to pain and loss. When we suffer, we often find ourselves sinking in a sea of darkness. God becomes hard to find in that darkness, and our trial of pain becomes a crisis of faith. Don Baker shares these insights about the link between suffering and doubt:

> Pain speaks a strange language—it plays funny tricks on us. It makes us think things and say things and even believe things that are not true. When pain begins to bore its way through human flesh and on into human spirit and then just sit there and hurt and hurt and hurt, the mind becomes clouded and the brain begins to think strange things like—*God is dead* or *He's gone fishing* or *He's just plain not interested.* [3]

I have to confess that there are times when I wrestle with the deep mysteries of God. It's not that I any longer question His existence; that fact has been settled in my heart. Nor do I any longer question the reality of the Resurrected Christ in my life; He is my Friend, and the greatest reality and truth in my life. I no longer question whether God loves me unconditionally; I'm secure in the knowledge that love and forgiveness are inextricably part of His nature. There have been times early in my pilgrimage of faith when I struggled with these issues, but no longer; they are settled for me.

Yet there's one area of faith where I confess I still struggle: the area of God's omnipotence. It's a struggle I've faced many times, such as when I've officiated a funeral for a little child or when I've stood in a famine-ravaged village in Africa. I felt it keenly when my brother died at the age of forty-one. During my time of grieving for Paul, I've had a genuine and continual experience of the presence and grace of God—yet at the same time there is a deep disappointment that God would allow him to get cancer and die. In these days, I've had to honestly ask God, "Are You really all-powerful? If You're really all-loving and all-powerful, then why have You allowed Paul to suffer and die?"

Doubts such as these can have a paralyzing effect on our faith. We can begin to focus on our doubts so completely that we can become incapable of functioning. It was Shakespeare who wrote in *Measure for Measure*, "Our doubts are traitors, and make us lose the good we oft might win by fearing to attempt." This is an accurate assessment of the power of intense doubting to immobilize us. How can we be healed of the paralysis that doubt so often causes?

We need to understand that God calls us to a kind of faith that leaves no part of our lives untouched. Biblical faith must touch the mind, the heart, and the will. If our faith is only an intellectual kind, then we'll probably never move beyond our doubts and questions.

The proof that our faith has touched our *hearts* is in the way we love and care for people in the name of Jesus Christ. At the end of Matthew 25, Jesus describes a time of judgment that awaits us, and in this great final exam of the Christian life, we won't be asked any questions about doctrinal knowledge or our orthodoxy. The quiz we will have to answer is this: "When people were starving, did you feed them in My name? When they were thirsty, did you give them drink? When they were alone and friendless, did you befriend them? When they were ill-clad or sick or in prison, did you go to them and meet their needs in My name?" That, says Jesus, is the test of whether our hearts have been touched by our faith.

The proof that our faith has touched our *will* is in the way we live increasingly more obedient and courageous lives for Christ, willing to step out and risk for Him, willing to *act.* C. S. Lewis illustrates this truth for us in *The Screwtape Letters* as he depicts the senior devil Screwtape advising the junior devil Wormwood to lure his human "patient" (a Christian whose faith Wormwood is seeking to subvert) into inaction. "No amount of piety in his imagination and affections will harm us," says Screwtape, "if we can keep it out of his will." [4]

Not long ago, I stood in the dusty streets of a little African village called Goram Goram in the country of Burkina Faso (formerly Upper Volta). This village had suffered for years from ground-cracking drought and famine, followed by sudden rains and flooding. All the mud huts of the village had been destroyed. Now cholera plagued these homeless, devastated people.

During my time in Goram Goram, I held little children in my arms who were dying of malnutrition and childhood diseases that would have been easily treatable in the United States. And at the end of the day, I would just go to my knees and ask, "Why, Lord? How can there be so much needless suffering in this place? If You are all-loving and all-powerful, Lord, why does this happen?" And in my helplessness before all the tragedy I had witnessed, I often felt totally overwhelmed, and tempted to immobility and despair.

I finally had to pray, "Lord, I'm going to have to yield this tragedy to You. I don't understand why You've allowed all this suffering, but I can't take it all onto myself. Lest I become immobilized by my depression and my questioning, I'm going to have to yield the Why of this situation to You. I refuse to give in to the paralysis of doubt. I'll do all I can to help while I'm here, and then I'll tell this story to my friends back home. But the incomprehensible Why I surrender to You."

The questions I asked God on my knees in Goram Goram are the oldest and hardest questions human beings have ever asked. They're the same questions Job asked in his crisis of suffering. Throughout the book of Job, he probes God deeply with such questions as, *Are You all-powerful, and are You in control? Are You just? Are You loving? If You are, then why do You allow the innocent to suffer?* By the end of the book, Job finally comes to a place of acceptance and peace with his doubts.

But it's important to understand that God *never* answers Job's questions. God never tells Job *why* he suffered. We wonder why, don't we? And we identify with Job. When we face illness or loss or the end of life itself, we want to know why. We implore God with our questions, but the sky is silent.

We think, "Well, God *owes* me an explanation!" And then we immediately realize, "And yet, if He is really the sovereign God of the Universe, He really doesn't owe me anything." But then we think, "Well, if He's a God of love, then doesn't He *want* me to understand the reason for my suffering?" And to these questions, I have to answer, *Yes,* I believe God does want us to understand—at least to the extent we *can* understand.

Yet we are finite beings seeking to understand the ways of an Infinite God. It may well be that if God gave us the answers to all our questions, we wouldn't be able to comprehend them. The problem of suffering is one of the deep mysteries of the universe, as impenetrable to our minds as quantum physics. We have to acknowledge with Paul that all we can grasp is a poor reflection in a dark and imperfect glass. One day we shall see face to face, and we shall know fully—but for now we know only in part.

In the end, our hardest questions will remain unanswered. Our reasoning and questioning of God can take us, perhaps, 90 percent of the way toward a settled assurance and trust. But we're going to have to take that other 10 percent *by faith.* Not "blind faith," but a faith that proceeds from an honest quest for truth. I affirm these words of Ralph Waldo Emerson: "All I have seen teaches me to trust the Creator for all I have not seen."

Will it ever end?

I think most of us, in the back of our minds, are vaguely hoping for that day in our walk with God when our faith has solidified like concrete, when we have no more doubts to trouble us. I don't believe that day will ever come, because I don't believe God intends for any of us ever to stop growing and learning.

But I am convinced we can come through our times of doubt and emerge into a faith that stands firmly, resolutely, and confidently. It was Francis Bacon who once wrote, "If a man will begin with certainties, he shall end in doubts. But if he will be content to begin with doubts, he will end with certainties." We can come to a haven of settled and secure faith. In fact, that is the goal of doubt: to strengthen our faith. For while it is no sin to struggle with doubt, it is certainly no virtue to prolong our doubting endlessly.

I've encountered some people who appear to take masochistic pleasure in endlessly questioning everything about their faith. They seem perversely proud of their continual doubting—and they never seem to arrive at a point of conviction and liberating assurance. God never intended this kind of perpetual turmoil to be the norm in the Christian life.

What can we do to come safely through a time of crisis in our faith? First, we need to *spend time in the Word of God.* Often, we respond to doubt by laying aside our Bibles and turning elsewhere for the answers to our questions. Yet, it is precisely at such times that we most need the companionship and wisdom of God's Word. J. I. Packer calls faith "the subjecting of mind and conscience to the Word of God." In *God Has Spoken,* he writes, "In the absence of certainty as to just what the Word of God is, superstition prevails, and instead of faith there is fog. . . . Doubts and uncertainties about God and our standing with Him are poor companions to live and die with; but many today are never out of their company, because they know of no assurances from God on which their faith may rest." [5]

Second, we need to *spend time in prayer.* You may be thinking, "Prayer! How can I pray when I am doubting so deeply?" But now is when you need prayer the most! James 1:5 tells us, "If any of you lacks wisdom, he should ask God, who gives generously to all without finding fault, and it will be given to him."

Yet as we look further in that passage we may become confused about the role of prayer in a time of doubt. James 1:6–8 tells us, "But when he asks, he must believe and not doubt, because he who doubts is like a wave of the sea, blown and tossed by the wind. That man should not think he will receive anything from the Lord; he is a double-minded man, unstable in all he does." Doesn't this verse say that any doubt at all is fatal to one's prayers? No, there's an enormous difference between people who struggle with questions about their faith and those who are "double-minded," "unstable," who allow themselves to be blown and tossed on a sea of perpetual doubting.

What God is saying to us through James is precisely what Jesus said in Mark 9, as He answered the plea of a father to heal his son. "Everything is possible," said Jesus, "for him who believes." And our prayer to God must echo that anxious father's reply: "I do believe; help me overcome my unbelief!" As we come to God in prayer, offering our doubts and asking for wisdom, we have to honestly confess to God, "I believe you, Lord—at least I believe you enough to come to you in prayer. But I also have to honestly confess my doubts. In fact, there are times when I'm not sure I really believe in you. But I'm asking you to help me overcome my doubts. Help me to have a deeper faith in you."

Third, we need to *act in obedience.* We need to commit our *will* to God even though our minds and emotions are in turmoil. You see, doubt is not the opposite of faith. The opposite of faith is *disobedience.* When we choose to be obedient to God, even as we are raising our questions and doubts, we are able to see more clearly that the process of doubting is really woven into the process of faith.

Matthew 14 tells of a time when Peter and his friends were out fishing on a lake, and a storm rose up and began to swamp their boat. Suddenly Peter saw Jesus walking toward them across the water. Peter was terrified; he couldn't believe it was really Jesus. "Lord," he called, "if it's really you, tell me to come to you on the water." Jesus' reply? "Come."

So Peter acted against the counsel of his doubts; he left the safety of his boat and stepped out in faith upon the water—and he began to *walk!* After a few steps, he paused to check out his circumstances. Seeing the wind and the waves, he suddenly realized that what he was doing was plainly impossible—and this realization began to *sink* him. As he started to go under, the Lord reached out to him and saved him.

We could all be a little more like Peter, stepping out in risky obedience, disregarding our doubts and circumstances. We may, like Peter, begin to doubt and get ourselves in deep water—but Jesus is always there to pull us up again.

Josh McDowell tells the story of a tightrope walker who came to town with the circus. Before an awed crowd of onlookers, he performed many daring feats—riding a bicycle, carrying chairs, walking on his hands, pushing a wheelbarrow—all on a tenuous span of rope hundreds of feet above a river. Finally, he came to his last feat. "I will now push this wheelbarrow across that rope with another person in it! Do you think I can do it?"

"Yes!" answered the confident crowd. "You can do it!"

"That's wonderful!" said the tightrope walker. "Then who among you wants to be first to volunteer as my passenger?"

Total silence.

"I'll volunteer," said a young woman, stepping confidently to the front. The crowd was amazed at her courage. The stuntman took her across the river in the wheelbarrow, then back again, all without a hitch.

Afterwards, someone ran to the young woman and asked, "Where on earth did you get the courage to do that? Weren't you scared to death?"

"Not at all," she smiled. "You see, the tightrope walker

is my *father*—and I've been performing that feat with him all my life."

And so it is with us. As we live according to our faith instead of according to our doubts, our faith and assurance grow. We come to know the Father *personally,* not just intellectually. Through our active daily reliance upon Him, we can finally reach a place where we can say, "I'm not afraid to trust my heavenly Father. I've been performing the feat of faith with Him all my life."

Accepting the mystery of God

Trembling and feeling very small, we come to God with our little portion of faith in our hands, and we lift it up to Him. And He smiles upon us, and we warm ourselves in His love. He takes that little portion of faith that we offer Him, and He blesses it—

And He *breaks* it. And He breaks it again. And again. And each time He breaks it, it multiplies before our wondering eyes. And He gives us back our enlarged and multiplied faith, and we feed on it, and we *grow.* As we grow, our vision of God becomes clearer and greater and more assured.

In *Prince Caspian,* the second volume of The Chronicles of Narnia, C. S. Lewis portrays a reunion between Aslan—the great golden lion who in many ways represents Christ—and a young girl named Lucy:

> A circle of grass, smooth as a lawn, met Lucy's eyes, with dark trees dancing all round it. And then—oh joy! For *He* was there: the huge Lion, shining white in the moonlight, with his huge black shadow underneath him. . . .
>
> She rushed to him. She felt her heart would burst if she lost a moment. And the next thing she knew was that she was kissing him and putting her arms as far round his neck as she could and burying her face in the beautiful rich silkiness of his mane.
>
> "Aslan, Aslan. Dear Aslan," sobbed Lucy. "At last.". . .
>
> "Welcome, child," he said.
>
> "Aslan," said Lucy, "you're bigger."
>
> "That is because you are older, little one," answered he.
>
> "Not because you are?"

"I am not. But every year you grow, you will find me bigger." [5]

I really identify with those words. Every year I grow, I seem to find that God is bigger in His goodness and love than I ever thought possible. The more we grow, the bigger God will seem. Our doubts, though they will continue to come, will seem less important, less of a hindrance. As we begin to see faith more as a commitment to a relationship than an assent to a creed, we will experience increasingly more of the reality of God. Even more, we'll discover that we don't need to understand everything about God in order to love Him.

We believe in the Almighty God of the Universe, the One who created heaven and earth, who spoke the billions of stars into existence, who so amazingly and wonderfully made us as human beings. Such a God could never be enclosed within the boundaries of our finite understanding. We can understand a great deal about Him, especially as He discloses Himself to us in His Word. But ultimately there must be aspects of His nature that we can only accept as Mystery for now. Our understanding can penetrate so far into that Mystery, and no further. Only a God who is great enough to inspire our doubts and questions could be great enough to inspire our faith.

8

Healing the Hurt
of Conflict

Conflict isn't necessarily good or bad. Conflict just is.

—David Augsburger

Blessed are the peacemakers,
for they will be called sons of God.

—Matthew 5:9

The gray chill of winter clung to him as he trudged up the snow-covered walk. His mood was as bleak as the word *divorce*. He mounted the steps to the front door and rang the doorbell of the house that used to be his home. A few moments later the door opened just a crack. "What do you want?" said the woman behind the door.

"I just came to pack my things. I won't be long."

The door opened wider and the woman stepped aside. The man entered, noting the lonely seeming Christmas tree in its usual corner of the living room. The ornamentation seemed half-hearted.

She eyed him coldly. "What are you going to pack your things in? Didn't you even bring a suitcase?"

"*You* got all the luggage," he replied bitterly, "along with the house, the refrigerator—"

"All right."

"—the stereo—"

"*All right!* Just take what you came for and get out! There are trash bags under the kitchen sink! I'll be in the bedroom, dumping your clothes out on the floor!"

He went to the kitchen. Muttering, he flung the cabinet

doors wide and began rummaging about for the trash bags. He spilled cleanser and sent a lightbulb wobbling across the floor. "I can't find them! Where did you—Oh, here they are."

As he strode down the hallway toward the bedroom, he turned over various phrases in his mind, searching for just the right words to hurt her as deeply as possible. When he was sure he was in earshot, he began, "Soon as I get out of here, I won't have to take any more of your—" He fell silent at the doorway.

She was kneeling on the floor in front of the dresser, surrounded by piles of underwear and socks. All the anger was gone from her face. She reached into the bottom of the open drawer before her and pulled out a little pair of blue jeans, and a small T-shirt with teddy bears on the front. Tears spilled down her cheeks as she clutched these reminders to herself— reminders of the little child who had passed through their lives a few short years before.

The man knelt beside his wife and pulled her close. Her head fell onto his shoulder and she began to sob. Then his tears began to fall, mingling with hers. "What are we doing?" he said at last. "God held us together when Timmy got sick— and even when he died. Can't He hold us together now?"

This moment of warmth in a cold, gray day was just the beginning, the first tentative step for two people on a long, uphill road to reconciliation. There were many painful memories to be healed, many hurtful words and acts to be forgiven. There were still many tears, recriminations and angry silences ahead for these two people—but there were also many embraces and words of love and repentance. The conflict of the past could never be undone—but it could be healed. It's never too late for faith, hard work, and love to bring a new beginning out of the deepest trial of conflict.

Surrender

Conflict can break relationships—but it can also *strengthen* them. It all depends on the choices we make in our trial of conflict. Whatever your conflict right now, God is calling you to learn to surrender—not necessarily surrender to the person who opposes you but surrender to God, and to His healing solution for your struggle. It takes two to make an argument, but it only takes *one* to make the healing choice, the positive response which results in healing for *both* people involved, the response that brings strength instead of destruction to a relationship.

You may have grown up in a home where continual conflict was the norm; you may believe "fighting it out" is the only way to face any conflict. Or you may come from a home where anger was suppressed, not expressed; conflict was avoided to such an extent that there was very little truth and openness in your relationships. When these are the only two options, there will inevitably emerge a winner and a loser—and the relationship between these two people will be damaged or broken. A choice between "fight" or "flight" is a choice between two forms of calamity: For whether we win our conflict through intimidation or lose through retreat and withdrawal, we have allowed an *opportunity* to turn into *tragedy*.

The good news the Bible offers us is that there is a *third* option for our trials of conflict: not winning, not losing, but *healing* the conflict. When we choose neither to fight nor to fold in a confrontation, then we can *grow* in our relationships with others. As we listen carefully and actively to the other person's views, we gain new insights and we learn to *act* on his concerns rather than simply *react* to his anger. We find validity in his arguments, and we test and strengthen our own views in the crucible of conflict.

The only true solution to the dilemma of conflict is the realization that conflict must not be won or lost, but *healed*—and the ultimate source of healing power for all our trials, including the trial of conflict, is God. Conflict that has been either won or lost is conflict that has been resolved by natural, human means. But a *healed* conflict has been resolved by *super*natural, *super*human means. The same Holy Spirit who comes into the Christian at the moment of conversion is there as a counselor, a confidant, a power source in times of conflict. He is there for us to draw upon in times of conflict, helping us reweave the fabric of our torn relationship.

But how do we draw upon the Holy Spirit during the heat of conflict? Conflict comes in so many ways. We may pick up the phone or answer the door to be surprised by a hostile confrontation. Or conflict may creep up on us imperceptibly, as a discussion with a friend gradually degenerates into a heated argument. Whether we fall into conflict suddenly or subtly, it's my experience that there's always time for a moment of silent prayer.

I confess that it's not always my first instinct to respond to conflict with prayer. But whenever I do, the outcome of the conflict is invariably far different than when I simply meet that confrontation in my own strength and wisdom. My prayer usually goes something like, "Lord, please fill me with the power and insight of the Holy Spirit. Give me Your words of peace and forgiveness to speak." I may have to pray this prayer repeatedly during the crisis as the temptation to respond in anger arises again and again. Prayer is surrender to God, and that surrender must be continuous.

Through prayer, God can empty us of our defensiveness, while filling us with Christlike qualities of humility and forgiveness. In reliance upon God, we can listen with sensitivity and speak the truth in love. Surrender to God is the true basis for a healing, loving resolution of our trial of conflict.

Glorious slavery

Mike and Susan were at odds, embittered and hostile toward each other. Their ten-year-old marriage was slowly being destroyed by continual conflict. Whenever Mike began to speak, Susan would interrupt with the words "Yes, but—" and go on to assert her defense. And Mike, not to be outdone, would soon interrupt in his own defense with the same words, "Yes, but—"

Susan: "Yes, but what about you? You're never home on weekends! You're always out rafting or skiing or—"

Mike: "Yes, but I've invited you to come along! You just never want to do the things I want to do—"

Susan: "Yes, but do you ever consider *my* feelings? Do you ever think of spending just one day a week doing something *I* like to do?"

Mike: "Yes, but the *only* things you like to do are going shopping or visiting your mother or—"

Susan: "Yes, but the only thing *you* ever want to do with me is—"

Mike: "Yes, but what do you do as soon as I want to show you a little affection? You pull back and—"

And on and on.

After a couple weeks of refereeing this kind of dialogue in my counseling office, I stepped in and said, "Mike, there are two things you need to begin doing, as I perceive it: First, you need to begin affirming Susan's self-worth and her value as your wife and the mother of your children. Second, you need to love her as Christ commanded you, to give her more of your evenings and weekends, and more of yourself."

"Yes, but—" came the predictable reply, "what about Susan?"

Then I said to Susan, "You know, Susan, you're not giving Mike any encouragement or sense of significance in his role as the husband-father in the home. You're also withdrawing all your affection and sexual interaction with him because you want to punish him until he becomes all you want him to be."

And, predictably, she replied, "Yes, but—"

And it continued that way for several more weeks. But finally, as the love of Christ began to seep deeper into their lives, it began to be not "Yes, but!" but *Yes:* "Yes! I see that now. Regardless of how my spouse responds, *my* response is my responsibility, and—Yes!—I want our marriage to be healed." And healing began to take place in this marriage.

In his book *Caring Enough to Confront,* David Augsburger writes,

> Nothing ends blaming games like the recognition that the blame must be scored 50–50. . . . If there is blame to be fixed, it includes both persons involved.
>
> It takes two people to have a problem. In a marriage, for example, neither I nor you is the whole problem. "We" are our problems. The trouble is with "us." Both people are involved in the hurt, the problem, the tragedy of a marriage in pain.[1]

The healing of our relationships and our conflicts begins when we stop saying, "Yes, but—" and start simply saying *Yes;* when we stop defending ourselves and blaming others, and begin taking ownership of our own failures and sins; when we recognize that our attitude is always ours to choose. The healing choice in a time of conflict is the decision to stop saying, "*You* make me angry," and to start saying, "*I'm* feeling angry about the problem between us. Let's focus our energy on solving the problem, not on hurting each other."

The healing choice doesn't come easily to us in times of conflict. As human beings we are fighters by nature. "What causes fights and quarrels among you?" asks James 4:1–2. "Don't they come from your desires that battle within you? You want something but don't get it. You kill and covet, but you cannot have what you want. You quarrel and fight. You do not have, because you do not ask God." Here, James addresses Christians—you and me—and he confronts the choice we so often make to create tension and conflict between ourselves and others. Our own sinful desires are at the root of much of the conflict we experience in life. We kill and covet, says James; we kill with our words, we kill with our thoughts, we kill with cruelty and accusation and sarcasm.

The Word of God confronts us head-on in our sin. We are to love unconditionally, even in the midst of conflict. The gospel, in the final analysis, is *slavery*—a glorious kind of slavery that ultimately leads to true freedom. The gospel binds us against our natural will to do what is *un*natural—and even what is *super*natural. The gospel constrains us to love.

In his New Testament letters, the apostle Paul continually calls himself a "slave" to Jesus Christ, and this is no mere figure of speech. To Paul, Jesus is Lord and Master, and that means Paul surrenders to Him all rights, including the right to defend himself, the right to resentment, the right to revenge. At the heart of our slavery to the gospel is unconditional, volitional love.

In marriage, unconditional love is expressed in *commitment.* Often when a Christian husband and wife come to me for counsel, they tell me their romantic love is fading and they are falling deeper and deeper into conflict. At such times I encourage them as two people who have placed themselves under the lordship of Christ to see themselves as *slaves.* I show them in the Scriptures that the command of their Lord and Master is to *love one another.* It's amazing how much harder we work at our marriages once we have accepted this fact.

To love unconditionally means to love *even when we don't feel like loving.* And you may wonder, "Well, isn't it really hypocritical to love when I don't feel like loving?" No, there's nothing hypocritical in acting in ways you don't *feel;* hypocrisy is the sin of acting in ways you don't *believe.* When we truly commit ourselves to loving others as Christ commanded, then we will be sincerely and obediently living out our Christian beliefs—whether we *feel* like it or not. God calls us to love in unlovely situations, to show kindness to enemies, to bless those who curse us. The amazing thing is that as we love when we don't feel like loving, often the feelings return as well.

"Ungraceful people"

Who is the most "ungraceful" person in your life right now? Who is that one person who seems to communicate to you a total lack of understanding of the grace of God? Someone probably comes very readily to mind.

Your "ungraceful person" may in fact be a fellow Christian. In *Of God and Men,* A. W. Tozer describes these "ungraceful" Christians: "Unsaintly saints are the tragedy of Christianity. People of the world usually pass through the circle of disciples to reach Christ, and if they find those disciples severe and sharp-tongued they can hardly be blamed if they sigh and turn away from Him." [2] You've probably encountered some of these "unsaintly saints." They are genuine Christians, people who have received the grace of God—yet they seem to have no understanding of the fact that they have been called by God to *show* that same forgiving grace to others.

Then again, your "ungraceful person" may be someone who is indifferent or even hostile to God. You may actually be experiencing conflict with this person *because* you are a Christian, and your "ungraceful person" feels confronted by the evidence of God's grace in your life.

Your "ungraceful person" is the one who always takes the opposite point of view; the one who tends to be cynical and sarcastic; the one who continually rubs you the wrong way; the one who never says, "I'm sorry" or "I was wrong" or "please forgive me"; the one who is insensitive to your feelings, your beliefs, and your needs. Your "ungraceful person" may even be a member of your own family.

Josh McDowell's "ungraceful person" was his own father.

In *Evidence That Demands a Verdict,* he writes that his father "epitomized everything I hated. . . . He was the town drunk. My high school friends would make jokes about him making a fool of himself around town. . . . Sometimes when we had company I would tie Dad up in the barn and tell them he had to go on an important call." [3]

But when McDowell became a Christian, God's grace was able to transform his hatred for his father into *love.* A few months after his conversion to Christ, McDowell was injured in an automobile accident. His father came to visit him in his hospital room. At one point as they were talking together, he broke down and said, "Josh, I've been the worst kind of father to you. How can you love a man like me?"

"Dad," said McDowell, "six months ago I couldn't. But now, through Jesus Christ, I *can* love you." And he explained to his father the meaning of God's grace in his life. Before leaving that hospital room, Josh McDowell's father had committed his life to Jesus Christ. From then on he was a changed man. He put alcohol out of his life, and scores of people who saw the change in his life also came to know Jesus Christ. About a year later this changed man died at peace with God and at peace with his son.

That's what God's grace is all about: When you don't deserve love, you're loved. When you don't deserve forgiveness, you're forgiven. When your life seems no longer worth living, you're given a second chance—you're even given *new* life, *eternal* life. That's the grace of God, and everyone who has committed himself to Christ has received this undeserved kindness from God. God in His grace loved us while we were still His enemies, locked in rebellious conflict against His will. He loved us patiently, aggressively, continuously, even while we fought Him, until at last we surrendered and confessed to Him, "My Lord and my God!"

The ultimate test of the reality of God's grace in our hearts is our willingness to love the "ungraceful people" who come into our lives. Grace pursued us while we were still in rebellion against God, and grace calls us to reach out in love, acceptance, and forgiveness to our "ungraceful person." Grace calls us to respond to abuse and anger with patience and understanding. Grace calls us to be sensitive to the hurts and insecurities that so often underlie the abrasiveness of our "ungraceful persons," to look beyond the irritation to the *need* of that person.

In our own lives there will be times when our "ungraceful persons" will be changed and won over as we patiently model the grace of God toward them. But there will be other times when there will be no change, no reconciliation, no happy ending. If that is your trial right now, I know there is great pain in that. I've known that pain in some of my own relationships.

But you *do* have one promise for your trial of conflict, even when it seems your "ungraceful person" has hardened his heart against you and will *never* change—the promise that God's grace is sufficient in your life, even for the hurt of conflict that won't go away. It's the same promise God made to Paul in his trials: "My grace is sufficient for you, for my power is made perfect in weakness" (2 Cor. 12:9). God has promised to supply His strength for your weakness, and His grace for your "ungraceful person."

An allegiance to relationships

Jesus said, "Blessed are the peacemakers"—but He didn't mean we are to seek peace at any price. There are some issues that *demand* we take a stand, for to do any less would be disobedience to God: the centrality of Christ, and His sacrifice for our sin; His bodily Resurrection; the absolute authority of Scripture; salvation by grace through faith, apart from works; the reality of eternal life with Christ for all who believe in His name; the Great Commission of the church to claim, train, and send people into the world for Christ; the absolute demand of God on our lives that we love Him with all our heart and strength, and that we unconditionally love one another. These are unbendable truths, and we must stand firm on them.

We are to stand for the truth, but as Ephesians 4:15 tells us, we must speak the truth *in love.* Christian peacemaking is a truthful, positive, aggressive ministry of bringing divided people together into a healed relationship. Christian reconciliation takes place only as we face our conflicts and work through them to a point of true understanding and acceptance. We may not always reach total agreement with our opponents, but we can weather our conflicts with our capacity to love one another intact—and even strengthened.

I've found that in time people will either develop an allegiance to issues or an allegiance to relationships. So if we don't make the healing choice to make relationships our priority, then we will gradually become more and more exclusively committed to issues, and the unconditional love of Christ will be choked out of our lives. A true Christian peacemaker genuinely cares about issues—but he cares even *more* about relationships.

Once when I was in high school, three of my friends and I were going to the drive-in at the edge of town, and each of us had a date for the evening. So there were eight of us in our family car, an old Ford Fairlane. My friend Pedro Garcia was one of the eight people in the car that night. In fact, his presence was *keenly* felt that evening because Pedro is 6' 5" and weighs about 220 pounds.

About a half-hour into the movie, Pedro said, "It's too crowded in here. My date and I are going to get out and sit somewhere else." So he and his date got out and walked around for a while, and they finally decided that the best seat in the place was atop the roof of our Ford Fairlane. So Pedro and his date (who was not particularly petite either) got on top of our car. About half-way through the movie, the rest of us in the car felt something coming down on our heads: the roof of the car, sinking under the combined weight of Pedro and his girlfriend. The rest of us sat through the remainder of the movie hunched down in our seats.

Driving home, I knew I had some explaining to do. So I pulled in the drive, went in the house and told my Dad what happened. He looked out the window at the car in the drive and saw that the roof was caved in exactly as I had described it. I'll never forget the first words he said to me at that point: "Ron, you know I love you—"

Naturally, he had a good deal more to say—in fact, it was a fairly comprehensive discourse on the subject of the economic implications of auto body repair. But the *first* thing he said was, "Ron, you know I love you." In other words, he was telling me, "Ron, our relationship is more important than this issue. I love you more than that bashed-in Ford out there."

How are you doing at communicating that *people* are more important than the issues you confront? How are you doing at maintaining a priority of *relationship* with others in your family, your friendships, and your church?

The best place to work through conflict is not on our feet, with our jaws set and our fists doubled up, but on our knees— pleading for understanding, weeping over our sins, praying for the wisdom and unity of the Holy Spirit. "Blessed are the peacemakers," says the Lord, "for they will be called the children of God." The approval and blessing of God rests upon those who gently, humbly, lovingly speak the truth in love.

Unity in diversity

Some time ago, I received a call from a friend, an elder in another church. He was weary, exasperated, and there was a note of defeat in his voice. He told me he had been up until 2:30 in the morning in a long, hard meeting with the church board. This respected and influential evangelical church had now broken into bitterly divided factions.

How had this happened?

In talking further with my friend, I found that his church had fallen into an all-too-familiar pattern: Personalities had grown into parties. Convictions had degenerated into contentions. Rich diversity had been perverted into ugly division by an unloving, unyielding spirit. People had ceased to think of themselves as "one people" and instead aligned themselves into manipulative factions—"our people" versus "those people."

Ephesians 4:1–16 tells us that all Christians are called to unity and peace in the Holy Spirit. We have *one* hope, *one* faith, *one* Lord—and yet God has deliberately created the church to be richly *diverse* so that the greatest good can flow to the most people. Tragically, we often take the very diversity that God gave us for the sake of building the church and we set one part of the church against another, destroying each other and the work of God.

Where there is diversity there will be conflict. That is only natural, and conflict should not be avoided or papered over. We need to learn to *use* conflict in a way that brings about healthy growth and change, and an appreciation of other points of view.

Diversity can be our greatest strength in the church, as we move out in power and bold witness, changing lives and impacting the world for Jesus Christ by every possible means. But our diversity can *destroy* us if we begin to see one another as rivals instead of partners; if we begin living out a spirit of suspicion and competition rather than humility and gentleness; if our allegiance to *issues* becomes stronger than our allegiance to *relationships.*

John and I graduated from seminary together. Shortly after our graduation, John took his first pastorate in a small church in the Midwest. He had only been in that church a short time before a series of major conflicts developed, principally between himself and an elderly gentleman in the church. John wanted to bring in some newer kinds of music; the older man opposed it. John wanted to start some new forms of outreach and ministry to youth and adults; the older man opposed it. There was conflict in this church—conflict born of a diversity of opinions and gifts and approaches to ministry.

And yet there was a special dimension to the conflict in this church. These two men who were in such frequent and sharp conflict together were also best friends. They played golf together. They had fellowship together in each others' homes, sharing dinner and conversation and prayer together. This puzzled many people within and outside the church: How could these two men, divided as they were over so many issues, be such close friends?

One of the members of the church was talking with this elderly gentleman one time and asked, "I don't understand. You and John differ on just about every major issue in the church, and yet you seem to be such close friends. How can that be?"

"Oh, that's not so hard to understand," the old man replied. "Remember when John first came to our church? My wife was dying and this young pastor, whom we just barely knew at the time, came over to our house and sat by her bedside for twenty-four hours straight. He just held each of our hands in both of his and waited with us and prayed with us until morning came and my wife passed on into eternity. And then John just put his arm around me and wept with me. So, you see, we can differ over a lot of things, but the love of Jesus covers all those differences."

Issues are not our center. We have one center, one focus, one Lord: Jesus Christ alone. Our allegiance must not be to issues, but to *relationships*—first our relationship to Christ, and then our relationship to one another. When we are centered in Christ, then there is *unity* at the center of all our diversity, and over all our conflicts there is love.

Iron sharpens iron

God is not merely building individuals; He is building His church, the body of Christ, as an integrated whole. Each part must relate to all the other parts in order for the body to function properly. We cannot be all God intends us to be if we are isolated from other Christians, nor can we be whole in Christ if we are broken in relationship to other Christians— for together we *are* the body of Christ.

Proverbs 27:17 tells us that in the same way that iron sharpens iron, so do two friends sharpen each other. The image here is of a sword being honed and tempered for keen-edged strength. The sharpening process means *friction;* it means grinding off whatever impedes the efficiency and usefulness of the sword, whatever keeps the sword from being keen and sharp. Christian friends "sharpen" one another by telling each other the truth. The truth, expressed in love, makes us keen, sharp, useful tools in God's hands.

But truth often brings with it *conflict*—and that is why truth must always be accompanied by unconditional love, the kind of love that says, "No matter what you do or say, I will always accept you. I will always uphold you, and I will always try to build you up." Unconditional love gives unconditional affirmation.

A sword-edge that is mercilessly ground down or beaten with a sledge-hammer will not be sharpened; it will be *destroyed.* So it is with people and relationships. Unsparing truthfulness without love only serves to beat people down. But if we spend most of our time in our relationships giving encouragement and affirmation to others then we will have earned the right to be truthful at those times when the truth has to hurt in order to help.

In Galatians 6:1 Paul tells us, "Brothers, if someone is caught in a sin, you who are spiritual should restore him gently. But watch yourself, or you also may be tempted." There will probably be times in your life when you observe a fellow Christian slipping into a pattern of living which is harmful to himself or others. At such times, says Paul, it is our Christian duty to go to that person and gently confront him in love. Our goal in such situations is not merely to rebuke but to *restore*— and the restoration process can often be hard. Sometimes love calls us to confront. Caring often draws us into conflict. In *Caring Enough to Confront,* David Augsburger observes:

> Wholesale approval of another suggests that one is either totally unconcerned or radically uninvolved with the other. Cheap approval can be lavished on anyone at any time to any extent. But caring requires that one get interested in the direction the other's life is taking and offer real immediate involvement.
>
> If you love, you level. If you value another, you volunteer the truth.[4]

God's Word calls us to humility in our relationships with others, and warns "watch yourself, or you also may be tempted." Aware of our own fallibility, we can easily overlook the small slights and errors of others; we can confront with tears and sorrow instead of accusations; we can *accept* and *embrace* the erring brother or sister, knowing we too can fall into equally serious sin.

In all our relationships, there will be some honest differences, there will be misunderstandings, there may even be feelings of distrust and anger. Through it all, God in Romans 14:19 calls us to "make every effort to do what leads to peace and to mutual edification." And that word "peace" in the original New Testament Greek doesn't mean a cease-fire or an absence of conflict; rather it suggests a quality of being bonded and fused together in relationship with one another. That's the only truly healing choice for the hurt of conflict: to aggressively pursue real peace, reconciliation, and mutual upbuilding in all our relationships.

It takes a great deal of courage to make the healing choice in times of conflict—and all the more so since there is no guaranteeing the response of the other person in our conflict. "If it is possible, *as far as it depends on you,*" says Romans 12:18 (italics added), "live at peace with everyone." Our response is our responsibility; the other person's response is between him and God. But by the grace of God, we will seek

His approval and be His peacemakers in times of conflict.

A few years ago at a conference sponsored by the Fellowship of Christian Athletes, I met three young athletes who had come from the same small town in the Midwest. They had given their lives to Jesus Christ as Savior and Lord at this conference, and then they went back to their hometown with a burden to begin an evangelistic Bible study among their fellow athletes.

After the first meeting of this Bible study, these three young men went out for pizza, each wearing his F.C.A. T-shirt with a large cross on the front. They were sitting at a table eating pizza and drinking Cokes when a number of black-jacketed members of a motorcycle gang swaggered loudly through the front door.

Seeing the young athletes with their Bibles and the Christian insignia on their T-shirts, these bikers decided to have some fun. Laughing, pointing fingers, and swearing obscenely, the gang members circled the table of the three young athletes, who found themselves outnumbered more than three-to-one. One of the gang members began to bow mockingly, and said, "Hail to you, lovers of Jesus! Hail to you, Jesus-lovers!" His comrades began taking up the chant.

One of the Christian young men stood and leveled his gaze at the pack-leader. Nothing was said for a few moments, and the tension in the place was electric. The owner of the restaurant began to mentally calculate the damages from the fight that now appeared inevitable. Then the young athlete said with utter sincerity, "I want to thank you men for paying me the greatest compliment I've ever received. Thank you for calling me a lover of Jesus Christ."

The biker was dumbstruck. A tense confrontation had been turned into a bold but peaceful witness for Jesus Christ.

Has anyone ever paid you the compliment of *accusing* you of being a lover of Jesus Christ? When Jesus is the focus of all our desires, when He is the model for our character, when people are more important to us than issues, then God can take our trials of conflict and *transform* them into something beautiful and holy. That's the healing choice you can always make, no matter who opposes you, no matter how tough your struggle: the courageous *decision* to become a channel of God's unconditional love and grace to others, even in the crisis of conflict.

9

Healing the Hurt of Mistreatment

Jesus knew that the old eye-for-an-eye philosophy would leave everyone blind. He did not seek to overcome evil with evil. He overcame evil with good. Although crucified by hate, he responded with aggressive love.

—Martin Luther King, Jr.

Bless those who persecute you; bless and do not curse.

—Romans 12:14

Karl and Edith Taylor [1] had been married for twenty-three years. Edith considered herself "the luckiest woman on the block" to be married to such a loving, thoughtful man. In his job with the government Karl often had to go out of town, but he always wrote her faithfully and sent her a gift from every place he visited.

When Karl learned he was being assigned to Okinawa for a few months, the Taylors were saddened. It would be a long separation, but to keep their spirits up they made plans to put a down payment on a cozy little cottage-with-a-view just as soon as Karl returned.

So Karl went to Okinawa, and Edith was thrilled when his thoughtful cards and letters began to arrive. There were no gifts this time, but Edith knew her husband was putting every spare cent into savings for their dream house. Within a few weeks, however, the letters became fewer and briefer. Then, just as she was beginning to prepare for his return, Edith received word from Karl that he would have to stay three more weeks. Later, he wrote "just one more month." Then, "a couple months longer."

Finally, after Karl had been gone over a year, Edith received

147

the letter that shattered her heart. It began, "Dear Edith, I wish there were a kinder way to tell you we are no longer married. . . ." Karl had obtained a mail-order divorce from Mexico, and he was now married to a nineteen-year-old Japanese girl named Aiko.

Edith was devastated. The world ceased to make sense to her. There was no sound, no color, no taste anymore—only unrelieved pain. Finally, Edith took all her anguished feelings and honestly spread them out before God in prayer. As she wrestled with God, she realized she had a choice to make: she could become bitter and resentful, hating Karl for his betrayal and mistreatment of her—or she could choose to continue loving her husband. After a deep inner struggle, Edith made the healing choice for her trial of mistreatment: she wrote to Karl, told him she forgave him, and asked that they continue to keep in touch.

So for the next few years Karl and Edith exchanged cards and letters frequently. As time went by, Karl wrote Edith to tell her of his and Aiko's first child, a girl named Marie, then two years later another little girl named Helen.

A couple more years went by and Edith received another letter that broke her heart: Karl was dying of lung cancer. The medical bills were mounting, taking all the money Karl had saved to send his two little girls to school in America. Aiko and the girls would soon be left without anyone to provide for them. "What's going to happen to them now?" was the closing, despairing question of one of his letters.

Edith wrote back that she would like to pay the airfare to bring Marie and Helen to the States to live with her, if Karl and Aiko agreed. So a short time after Karl's death, fifty-four-year-old Edith Taylor became "the other mother" to a three-year-old and a five-year-old. A few months later, Edith arranged for Aiko to join her and the girls in America.

At the airport, Edith waited until the last person came off the plane—a thin, frail Japanese woman who seemed totally alone and afraid. Edith called Aiko's name, and they rushed into each other's arms. There they promised that together they would raise the girls for Jesus Christ. Edith Taylor later wrote, "Though Karl was taken from me, God has given me three others to love." She offered her trial of mistreatment to God, and God *transformed* her trial into healing for Aiko, Marie, and Helen—and for Edith herself. That's what God wants to do in our lives when we are victims of mistreatment.

The scales of justice

The normal human response to mistreatment is summed up by that bumper sticker we've all seen: "Don't Get Mad—Get Even!" Revenge is one of the oldest of human impulses. The stern existential philosopher Friedrich Nietzsche called revenge "the greatest instinct of the human race." Lord Byron wrote of "the sweetness of revenge." Francis Bacon called revenge "a wild justice."

When mistreated, our *natural* instinct is to choose the most hurtful words, to bring up old wounds, to do whatever we have to in order to balance the scales of that "wild justice" called revenge. But God has a better idea. It's not a *natural* solution to the hurt of mistreatment; it's a *supernatural* solution.

First Peter 2:19–20 tells us, "It is commendable if a man bears up under the pain of unjust suffering because he is conscious of God. . . . If you suffer for doing good and you endure it, this is commendable before God." Why do we receive God's approval when we endure mistreatment? The answer is in verse 21: "To this you were called, because Christ suffered for you, leaving you an example, that you should follow in his steps." Jesus committed no sin, yet He was insulted, tortured, and killed. He did not retaliate, He didn't threaten, He didn't get even. On the cross He modeled for us a kind of response to mistreatment that the world does not understand: "Father, forgive them." When we suffer mistreatment with patience and forgiveness, we are living after the example of Christ, following in His steps.

The attitude of the world is, "Why should I let someone insult me or hurt me—and then *forgive* him as if nothing ever happened?" But the attitude of the biblical Christian is, "I *must* forgive, even as I've been freely forgiven by God." Forgiveness is the grace that balances out the injustice of an unfair world. When another person acts unjustly toward us, the healing choice is to aggressively *forgive* that unjust treatment. We didn't deserve to be mistreated, nor does that person deserve to be forgiven—but when we choose to forgive, we counterbalance the other person's sin with the grace of God.

Yet it's so hard to let go of our resentment until we know that the score has been settled. Even when the one who hurt us has repented of his sin and asked forgiveness, it's still not always over for us. We've got the offender in the corner now, right where we want him. He's sinned and he knows it—and that gives us an edge. So we pile on a little guilt, a little blame, maybe do a little manipulating. If we're subtle, we'll use a few deftly chosen words here and there, carefully keeping the guilt feelings alive in the other person. And some of us aren't so subtle.

A few years ago, I was counseling a Christian husband and wife who were experiencing tremendous conflict in their marriage. Several years earlier, the wife had committed some very grievous sins against her husband. She had since repented of her sins, and some years had passed. Now, as their marriage was sinking toward dissolution, she said to me, "You know, it doesn't matter what we are arguing about—finances or our schedule or things that need to be done around the house—there isn't an argument we have on *any* subject that my husband doesn't bring up that one sin I committed years ago." The husband, sitting right next to her, just looked the other way. He couldn't deny it.

This is a marriage that will never truly *be* a marriage until the husband learns to forgive, finally and fully. So it is with you and me.

We're to forgive as we've been forgiven by God, love as we have been loved by God, give grace to others as we've received God's grace in our lives. As Christians, we're not only *saved* by grace but we're also called to *live* by grace. We are to impart God's grace to others—and especially to those who have mistreated us.

The power of forgiveness

I recently participated in a pastors' conference in Seoul, Korea. There I met a remarkable man, Dr. Kim Joon-Gon, National Director of Korea Campus Crusade for Christ. Dr. Kim survived the Communist persecution of the church during the Korean War, and today is one of the leading spokesmen for the amazing revival sweeping Korea. As we were having breakfast together one morning, he told me his story.

During the Korean War, Dr. Kim was in a Communist-controlled area for three months. One night, he was held by soldiers and forced to watch while his wife and parents were tortured and murdered by one Communist official. He himself was then beaten and left unconscious. He revived during the night, located his baby daughter—the only remaining member of his family—and escaped.

He was recaptured by the Communists and beaten again. Starving and suffering from massive injuries, Dr. Kim again faced the cruelty of the same Communist official who had murdered his family. During that time he went in and out of consciousness. He was so exhausted and defeated that he had ceased praying; he had lost all hope that God would answer. He was in total despair, a spiritual condition which he described to me as "the darkness of spiritual death, complete separation from God."

But even in his darkness, God was working in Dr. Kim's life. There came a moment in his suffering and hopelessness when he suddenly awoke to the realization that his lips were moving—and the words he spoke were words of *prayer.* "The Holy Spirit was speaking to me and through me," Dr. Kim said. "In that moment I had gone from death to life. I felt joy and peace spring up in my heart. The Lord had brought me through the valley of the shadow of death—and He was calling me to go and talk to the hated man who had murdered my family."

So Dr. Kim began to pray for his Communist persecutor—and as he prayed, he found new strength, new freedom, new life. Then he rose and went to this man and told him that he loved him, and that God loved him too. This Communist was startled at first to see that Dr. Kim was even alive—but he was absolutely thunderstruck when he heard this ragged, battered, half-dead prisoner begin to talk about the forgiveness of sin through Jesus Christ.

"This Communist leader could not believe I would come to him in love," Dr. Kim concluded. "He began to weep over his sins, and over the killing of my family. He committed himself to Jesus Christ and became a completely changed man from that day forward. Today that man is an elder in a church here in Korea, and he and I pray for each other every day."

Forgiveness is not just an idealistic notion for making people "nice." It's the hard-headed, realistic *demand* of God upon our lives. It's the power to change lives—and it's the only pathway to true inner healing when we have been severely, even brutally mistreated.

Our trial of mistreatment can be a destructive force in our lives—or it can be an *opportunity*. The choice is ours to make. When we are mistreated, we can seize the opportunity to demonstrate to others that Christ is *alive* in us, even in times of trial. Our lives can become a shining witness for Christ when we choose to respond in a supernatural, Christ-controlled way to the unfair treatment of others. We advance the kingdom of God whenever we endure persecution with *patience*.

Patience, remember, is the very first quality Paul attributes to Christian love in the famous "Love Chapter," 1 Corinthians 13. "Love is patient," he writes (or in your King James Bible, "Charity suffereth long"). Christian love, unconditional love, has a long fuse—and the first mark of a person who is growing in Christian maturity is that he is demonstrating more and more *patience* in his life, even when treated unfairly.

Displaying patience and love toward those who mistreat us doesn't mean we will let others walk all over us. There may be times when we will have to actively *respond* to those who unfairly treat us—but we will respond in an attitude of acceptance, gentleness, and love, not resentment or revenge. God may be calling us to firmly, patiently *confront* the offender about his sin for his own benefit, for the benefit of others whom he has hurt, or for the sake of a healed relationship between ourselves and the offender.

Self-defense

Everyone likes to get mail, and I'm no exception. I receive a lot of mail, and I enjoy reading every letter—well, almost every letter. Every few weeks I receive an anonymous letter harshly condemning something I've said or written, or judging my motives for something I've done. When I was younger, these anonymous critics could seriously wound me and even immobilize me.

One time a number of years ago I received a particularly

hurtful unsigned letter, and it made me stop and question *why* these cowardly attacks by unknown people could hurt me so deeply. Then it came to me: I wanted to *defend* myself—but I couldn't. I couldn't even find the person who wrote the letter.

Self-defense is our first instinct when we are mistreated. We want to be vindicated—but how can we ever defend ourselves against an anonymous critic or a false rumor or someone who shuns us and hurts us and refuses to tell us why? Against such trials of mistreatment, there just is no means of defense—but there is still a healing choice open to us: the choice to *stop* defending ourselves.

"We're all born with the desire to defend ourselves," A. W. Tozer once said, "and if you insist upon defending yourself, God will let you do it. But if you turn the defense of yourself over to God, He will defend you." There have been few things as helpful to me in my trials of mistreatment as this realization: *I don't have to defend myself.* Why? Because God has promised to be my Defender. In Exodus 23:22, He says, "I will be an enemy to your enemies and will oppose those who oppose you." And Psalm 72:4 says, "He will defend the afflicted. . . . He will crush the oppressor."

If defensive anger is our first instinctive response to mistreatment, then our next tendency is to nurture our initial anger into feelings of resentment and self-pity. Psychologists tell us anger that is not resolved turns into depression. If you have a tendency to become resentful and depressed when unfairly treated, James 5:8 (NASB) encourages you to "be patient; strengthen your hearts." That word "strengthen" in the original Greek conveys a sense of propping up or supporting something that is heavy. So if your heart is heavy when you have been treated unfairly, James says to let God support your heavy heart. Give your trial of mistreatment over to God, your Defender.

A slow-acting poison

He was an old man, approaching the end of his life. Tragically, he had chosen to grow old full of bitterness. He had become so eaten up by resentment over past injuries and injustices that it could be truly said that *bitterness* was the central pillar of his personality. His life was focused on complaining and rehearsing all the hurts of the past. He was soured on life, soured on people, and bitter toward God. His constant complaining was accompanied by insult and profanity. People hated to be around him.

This is not a description of one particular person, but a number of people I've known. You've probably known people like this too. How did they become so bitter? They didn't begin life with an attitude of resentment. In fact, the family and acquaintances of such people often talk with sadness about the *change* that took place in them over the years as they gradually became more sullen and closed.

Resentment is a slow-acting poison. It begins as we nurture those minor grudges, as we are slow to forgive, as we extract guilty apologies from others before we release them from our judgment. Bitterness takes root in our lives as we see someone who has mistreated us fall into misfortune—and we feel *good* about it. I know that feeling, and you probably do as well: that sinister joy we feel as we think, "He's getting just what he deserves!"

This grudge-bearing spirit is within each of us. If we give it the opportunity, this bitter, resentful spirit will wrap itself around our hearts and choke out all of our life and joy. It will eat us up inside, leaving us hollow and empty, capable only of hating and complaining and cursing the past.

A resentful, grudge-bearing spirit can drive us to do strange things. Not long ago a man was divorced by his wife and the court ordered him to pay a certain amount of alimony and child-support every month—and he grudgingly paid it in *nickels.* Every time his alimony and child-support payment came due, 160 pounds of nickels landed at his wife's door.

Another divorced man was ordered by the court to equally divide all the joint-property of his broken marriage with his ex-wife. He chose to do so with a chain-saw. As his neighbors looked on, he carefully measured the $100,000 suburban home that he and his wife had lived in for several years. When he found the precise mid-point of the home, he revved up his chain-saw and proceeded to cut his own home—floor, walls, ceiling, and roof—precisely in half.

These two men were driven to spectacularly strange forms of behavior because they allowed themselves to be eaten alive by resentment. But before we judge these men too harshly, we need to recognize that we too have that same spirit within us at times. We're usually just more subtle about it.

Resentment can come out at the most unlikely times—even in our prayer times together with other Christians. Others are sharing needs and concerns for intercession, and all the while we're mulling over some unfair treatment we've received. Finally it's our turn to share—and our "prayer request" is really a damaging word of gossip: "We really need to pray for Mary. She has such a problem with the way she treats people and really needs our prayers."

If you've begun to feed on past trials of mistreatment, then beware the tyranny of bitterness: if you're not careful, you'll grow old like that, and you'll die like that. If you don't begin *right now* to make the healing choice in your relationships, even when you are mistreated, then you'll leave a tragic legacy behind—the memory of a bitter, resentful person who just couldn't let go of the past and all that unfair treatment. The healing choice for the trial of mistreatment is the choice to forgive, and to let go of the past. Don't postpone that choice. Do your forgiving *now* so you can live a full, free, joyful life.

The 50:20 Principle

Ultimately we have to acknowledge that it's part of our Christian heritage to be mistreated and misunderstood. The Old Testament prophets were mistreated and killed. Jesus was rejected and crucified. The apostles and the Christians of the early church were martyred. Persecution of the church has taken place throughout the world from the first century to this very day—and it is growing worse, not better. As Paul tells us in 2 Timothy 3:12, "Everyone who wants to live a godly life in Christ Jesus will be persecuted."

You know what it means to be mistreated and misunderstood and so do I. In those times—in all the deep valleys and blue Mondays of my life—I've found encouragement in the biblical truth I call "The 50:20 Principle."

"The 50:20 Principle" comes from the last half of the book of Genesis, which tells the story of Joseph, the dreamer with the elaborate coat who was seized by his jealous brothers and sold into slavery in Egypt; Joseph was mistreated by his own family. The wife of Joseph's Egyptian master attempted to seduce him, slandered him, and had him thrown into prison; Joseph was mistreated by his employer. In prison, Joseph helped a friend, a fellow inmate, who later forgot Joseph and left him to languish in prison for two years; Joseph was mistreated by his friend.

There is probably no biblical figure more symbolic of the trial of mistreatment than Joseph. Yet as I have studied the account of his life from Genesis 37 to 50, I cannot find a single reference to any response of bitterness or resentment in Joseph's life.

By the end of Genesis, God has enabled Joseph to surmount all the episodes of mistreatment and betrayal in his life and he has become the governor of all Egypt. With the power of life and death in his hands, Joseph is now reunited with the brothers who years earlier had sold him into slavery. He has a golden opportunity to get even—and the brothers *know* it. With good reason, they now deeply fear the brother they had once cruelly mistreated. They plead for their lives and the lives of their families. They offer themselves as *slaves* to Joseph.

But Joseph doesn't take revenge. Rather, he *weeps*—then he says, "Don't be afraid . . . You intended it for evil, but God has used it for good." And there, in Genesis 50:20, we find "The 50:20 Principle," God's principle for responding to mistreatment: "You intended it for evil, but God has used it for good" (Genesis chapter *50, verse 20*). God had taken the evil and mistreatment that Joseph's brothers intended for him and transformed it into good. Genesis 50:20 is an Old Testament portrayal of the New Testament truth of Romans 8:28, the truth that God weaves together all the circumstances of our lives—even our trials of unfair treatment—into His good plan for our lives.

That's the principle I claim for my life whenever I have been treated unfairly. "You meant this mistreatment for evil, but I believe God is going to use even this for His ultimate good." In our trials of mistreatment, we don't need 20–20 vision, we need 50:20 vision—a vision which enables us to say, with peace in our hearts, "You meant it for evil, but God is going to use it for His good."

Such a response to the hurt of mistreatment goes against

our instincts. It's not going to come naturally. It's only going to come *supernaturally,* as we rely upon God and give our feelings of anger and resentment up to Him day by day, hour by hour, moment by moment.

The hurt of mistreatment puts the promises of God to the acid test. Unjust treatment is the crucible of our faith, testing just how serious we are about following Jesus Christ and living the life He led. The choice is ours: Are we going to insist on defending ourselves—or let God defend us? Are we going to let the past consume us—or are we going to let go of the past? We'll know we've made the healing choice for our trial of mistreatment when we can say, "I know you've meant it for evil, but God is going to use this—*even this!*—for His good."

10

Healing the Hurt of Fear

People of courage are also full of faith.

—Cicero

Even though I walk through the valley of the shadow of death, I will fear no evil, for you are with me.

—Psalm 23:4

The year was 1939. Dietrich Bonhoeffer, a thirty-three-year-old theologian from Breslau, Germany, paced the floor of his New York City apartment. A life-and-death decision loomed before him: Should he stay in the safety and security of America, or rejoin the persecuted Confessional Church in Nazi Germany, risking imprisonment and martyrdom? He fasted and prayed for wisdom.

A short time later, Bonhoeffer was on his way back to Germany. Against the pleading of his friends, he was determined to return home and take a bold stand for Christ against Hitler's tyranny. In 1943, he was imprisoned by the Gestapo, and later transferred to a succession of prisons and concentration camps. While in prison, he conducted worship services and encouraged his fellow prisoners. His ministry even extended to the prison guards, who were often heard to apologize to Bonhoeffer before carrying out some officially ordered act of cruelty.

One day in April 1945, as he was praying with the relatives of some men who had been executed, his captors took him away to be hanged. Just a few days before Allied forces liberated the death camp where he had been held, Dietrich Bonhoeffer died calmly, with a prayer of praise on his lips.

Why did he go back to Germany, knowing he risked persecution and martyrdom at the hands of the Nazis? Wasn't he afraid?

Bonhoeffer loved life, and he treasured its blessings: nature, music, art, books, and especially people. He had family, deep friendships, and a fiancée whom he loved dearly. He had everything to live for—but most of all, he lived for Jesus Christ. He believed it was not enough to serve his Lord through preaching and writing alone; he knew he had to live out his faith in costly obedience to God.

In one of his letters from prison, Bonhoeffer frankly confessed his fears, saying, "When I think of the worst that could happen to me, I find myself trembling." Bonhoeffer was afraid, but he subordinated his fear to his love for Jesus Christ.

Forty years later, the world came to know another man of bold Christian courage. The year was 1983. Benigno Aquino was returning home to the Philippines from the safety of exile in the United States. His friends, his wife, and his two daughters had tried to persuade him not to go, fearing he would be harmed or arrested, but he could not be dissuaded.

Aquino was an outspoken political opponent of Philippines' dictator Ferdinand Marcos, and had been a member of the Philippines Senate until he was jailed without trial in 1972. A moderate statesman caught in the vicious power struggle between left and right, Aquino was a lone voice pleading for the needs of the forgotten common people.

Aquino's plane, laden with reporters and concerned observers, landed at Manila International Airport and taxied to a stop. Philippine soldiers immediately boarded the plane and separated Aquino from the rest of his entourage, shoving him toward the door of the plane. Moments after he disappeared through the doorway, a volley of shots exploded outside the plane. Conflicting stories were later told about the next few agonizing seconds, but one fact was certain: Benigno Aquino was dead. His murder aroused outrage throughout the world—and it raised questions: "Why did he go back? Wasn't he afraid?"

Despite the intensive coverage this tragedy received from television, newspapers, and newsmagazines, the most compelling aspect of Aquino's story—his motive for going—was never disclosed by the news media. The truth is that Aquino returned to the Philippines for the same reason Bonhoeffer returned to Germany: his love for Jesus Christ.

In 1976, while still in a Philippines prison, Aquino had been given a copy of *Born Again* by Charles Colson,[1] and later saw a television interview in which the former Watergate defendant described his new life in Christ. For weeks before, Aquino had been so bitter and despondent that he was seriously contemplating suicide. But now, alone in his cell, Aquino suddenly felt the relentless love of God tugging at his heart—and he yielded himself to that love, committing himself to Christ.

Aquino was released from prison in 1980 so he could have emergency surgery in the United States—a stay which turned into a three-year exile in America. One day he was surprised to find himself on the same flight with Charles Colson. He introduced himself and shared how much Colson's testimony had meant to him while he was confined in prison. A friendship was immediately forged between them.

While in America, Aquino made a searching study of Dietrich Bonhoeffer's life—and it was the example of Bonhoeffer's courage that moved Aquino to begin his final trek home. "I consider Benigno Aquino a Christian martyr," Colson later told an interviewer, "because he had the courage to act on his beliefs. . . . The media glossed over his religious faith, and it explains everything about the man." [2]

What a glorious epitaph for any Christian, to have it said that our Christian faith explained *everything* about us. Ultimately it is only our love relationship with Jesus that enables us to make the healing choice for the hurt of fear.

The three opposites of fear

We have so many things to be afraid of these days. The things we read in the newspaper or see on television frighten us; surveys show that people who watch a great deal of television are generally more fearful than those who watch little or none at all. The threat of nuclear annihilation troubles our sleep. We fear crime, economic crisis, war, accident, illness, old age, natural disaster, and death—especially death. All of us have known the anxiety of wondering, "How will I endure the suffering of my death?" Many of us even dread what lies beyond the grave, and there is a paralysis in the fear of death that prevents us from being able to truly live.

"My heart is in anguish within me; the terrors of death assail me. Fear and trembling have beset me; horror has overwhelmed me." Those lines may sound like something out of Edgar Allan Poe, but they actually come from the heart of David, from Psalm 55. But Jesus never intended His own followers to be defeated by the hurt of fear. "Do not let your hearts be troubled," He told His disciples in John 14:1. "Trust in God; trust also in me."

That master psychologist of the first century, the apostle Paul, tells us that fear has not one but *three* opposites: (1) power, (2) love, and (3) inner wholeness ("a sound mind"). In 2 Timothy 1:7 (NKJV) he writes, "God has not given us a spirit of fear, but of power and of love and of a sound mind." Notice, first, that the person who is burdened with fear lacks *power;* he is powerless to dare great things for God. But the spirit we have received from God is one of boldness, courage, and power through the Holy Spirit.

Secondly, the person burdened by fear is not fully able to receive and give *love.* The fearful person is a guarded, wary person who seeks to be invulnerable and safe in his relationships. But the person who loves unconditionally is willing to take risks in relationships. He can't be afraid to be hurt; he must be prepared to be hurt again and again for the sake of loving others. God has not given us a spirit of fear, but of Christlike, unconditional love.

Finally, the person burdened with fear cannot experience *inner wholeness,* or soundness of mind and heart. He is unable to experience life fully because he is haunted by dangers, both real and imaginary. Like the security-obsessed fanatic who lives behind iron-barred windows and triple-bolted doors, surrounded by alarm systems and weapons and attack dogs, the fearful person one day awakes to find himself in a prison of his own making. God didn't give us a spirit of fear, but of a sound mind and a whole personality.

God seeks to turn our fears inside out and transform them into healing for others who are afraid. "Strengthen the feeble hands, steady the knees that give way; Say to those with fearful hearts, 'Be strong, do not fear; your God will come . . . to save you,' " says Isaiah 35:3–4. And in 1 Thessalonians 5:14 we're urged to "encourage the timid" and "help the weak." God calls us to make the healing choice to encourage those around us who are fearful.

Life without a net

"Living in the lap of luxury isn't bad," the late Orson Welles once said, "except that you never know when luxury is going to stand up." This is an apt restatement of Proverbs 23:5— "Cast but a glance to riches, and they are gone, for they will surely sprout wings and fly off to the sky like an eagle." Through the accumulation of wealth—investments, real estate, Individual Retirement Accounts, pensions, and Social Security—we seek to insulate ourselves from all risk by the time we reach retirement age. We want to be safe and secure, free from all worry and uncertainty. And thus we put our trust in the goods of this world, which could "take flight" at any moment.

And just as there is no security in wealth, neither is there security in health. I'm something of a fitness fanatic. I run two or three miles every day. I do aerobics with my children at the YMCA once a week. I enjoy anything physical—swimming, basketball, tennis, soccer, touch-football. I take a handful of vitamins every day, and carefully watch the food I eat. But no matter how well we take care of ourselves and try to minimize stress and risk in our lives, our health can disappear in a instant through accident or disease.

Our lives are balanced on a tightrope. We're living life without a net. The sooner we acknowledge this truth, the sooner we can begin investing in the real health and wealth that lasts eternally. That is why Jesus tells us in Matthew 6:31–33, "Do not worry, saying, 'What shall we eat?' or 'What shall we drink?' or 'What shall we wear?' For the pagans run after all these things, and your heavenly Father knows that you need them. But seek first his kingdom and his righteousness, and all these things will be given to you as well."

If you're a follower of Christ, then the only choice you can make is to seek your security in God's kingdom and His righteousness. But if you're not committed to Jesus Christ right now, then you've got to play it safe. You've got to base

your life on the false security of the things of this world—
even though striving to save your life will ultimately cost you
everything, *including* your life. As Jesus said, "Whoever wants
to save his life will lose it, but whoever loses his life for me
and for the gospel will save it. What good is it for a man to
gain the whole world, yet forfeit his soul?" (Mark 8:35).

Following Christ means counting the cost and accepting
the risks of being His disciple. God calls Christians out of
the temporal security of the things of this world to the ultimate
security of those things that will last for eternity. When that
is our security, we're free to wager all we are and have on
the promises of God.

Risky obedience

It is said that one of the chief functions of fairy tales is
to illuminate our darkest fears. This is certainly true of
J. R. R. Tolkien's *The Hobbit.* Tolkien, a close friend of C. S.
Lewis, wove stories that are rich in the truths of the Christian life.

Tolkien's hobbits are easy-going folk about three or four
feet tall. The average hobbit lives a well-ordered, sheltered
life in a quiet, comfortable hole in the ground. One day, a
fellow named Gandalf comes calling on a hobbit named Bilbo,
inviting him along on an adventure he is arranging. Bilbo is
aghast. "We hobbits are plain quiet folk and have no use for
adventures!" he replies. "Adventures are nasty disturbing un-
comfortable things! Make you late for dinner! I can't think
what anybody sees in them." ³

Isn't this a lot like the reply we make to God as He calls
us to the adventure of the Christian life? Tolkien has something
to teach us about fear in this story. He allows his hobbits—
symbolic of plain, ordinary people like you and me—to be
drawn into a harrowing, thrilling adventure. Ultimately, the
obedient courage of a few lonely, fearful hobbits enables a
kingdom to be saved from a terrible evil.

The adventure of the Christian life is like that: a journey
of risky obedience as we trust God to accomplish His victory
through our weakness, despite our fears and our trembling.
God uses the weak and fearful things of this world—hobbit-
hearted Christians like you and me—to tear down the strong-
holds of evil and declare salvation to a dying world.

Helen Keller was right when she said, "Life is either a grand adventure, or it's nothing." How it must break our Savior's heart to see so many of His people going to church every Sunday, singing bold hymns like "Onward Christian Soldiers" and "A Mighty Fortress Is Our God," claiming to trust in God—yet basing their lives on the false security of this world.

The freedom of risk

St. John Chrysostom (A.D. 347–407), the Archbishop of Constantinople during the reign of the Empress Eudoxia, understood the meaning of Christian courage. One day, he was commanded to appear before the Empress. "I hear you preach most ardently," she said, "that this man Jesus is Lord."

"I do," said Chrysostom.

"This teaching cannot be tolerated," Eudoxia replied, "for the only lordship recognized in Constantinople is that of this Throne. If you continue to preach these myths, then you will be banished from your home."

"Banish me? Why, the whole world is my home," said Chrysostom. "My Lord has said, 'Blessed are the meek, for they shall inherit the earth.' "

"I tell you that I am your ruler, not this crucified Jew!" said the Empress, her eyes flashing. "I will order all your treasures confiscated if you persist in calling this Jesus your 'Lord.' "

"You cannot take my treasures from me," he replied, "for I have hidden all my treasures in Heaven, where the Lord has promised that no one may break in and steal."

"You will cease calling this dead man your 'Lord'!" retorted Eudoxia, rising to her feet and shaking with rage, "or I shall confine you alone and friendless in the blackest pit in my dungeon!"

"That is impossible," Chrysostom gently replied, "for Jesus, my risen Lord, has promised, 'I will never leave you nor forsake you.' "

"Still you defy me!" shrilled the Empress. "Don't you know I have the power to order your *life* taken from you?"

"You have no power to take my life," he softly replied, "My life is hidden with Christ in eternity. If you slay me, I shall live again."

And the witness of history is that the Empress Eudoxia was frustrated in her attempt to force Chrysostom to deny the Lordship of Jesus. Ultimately, she deposed him and exiled him from Constantinople—but she was never able to silence him or intimidate him. What do you do with a man like John Chrysostom? He is *free!*

True freedom lies in *risk.* Your safety is your prison. If you knew what the future held, it wouldn't take any faith to live it. Our prayer before God should not be, "Lord, give us safety," but, "Lord, *increase our risks!* Give us boldness! Help us to dare great things for you!"

A few years ago, Bruce Larson was talking with the noted Christian counselor and physician, Paul Tournier. Larson asked Dr. Tournier how he was able to help his patients get rid of their fears. "Oh, I don't," Tournier quickly replied. "That which does not frighten does not have meaning. All the best things in life have an element of fear in them." I've seen this truth proved again and again: A life that is insulated from risk and fear is a life without meaning.

If we don't risk, we won't change. And if we don't change we won't grow, and we won't become conformed into the image of Christ. But it's our nature to resist change, isn't it? Even though our past has been unproductive and unfulfilling, most of us would rather return to the dreary security of the past than face the adventure of tomorrow. We're like the Israelites in the time of Moses, who wanted to return to the slavery of Egypt rather than trust God to lead them toward the Promised Land. We long for the bygone days when things were easier, when there was less pressure, when things were more familiar. We dig in our heels and say, "Let's camp here. Let this be my Mecca, my comfort zone."

I've heard that soon after a baby elephant is born, the animal trainer will chain him to a sturdy tree. The baby elephant will do all he can to get free, pulling and pulling on the chain until he is worn out. Finally he will begin to walk in a slow circle around that tree.

Over time, the elephant will continue testing his chain—but with decreasing persistence: just a tug on the chain, and then he gives up and begins walking around and around the tree. Eventually the elephant becomes so conditioned to his chain that the trainer no longer attaches it to the tree. He simply drops the chain on the ground—and the elephant will circle hour upon hour around that chain. The elephant is free to go anywhere—and he doesn't even know it. He's enslaved by the chains of the past.

We're so much like that elephant: we're completely free in Christ, yet we're enslaved by the chains of the past. There's an adventure waiting for us—but we prefer the same old familiar path, even though it only leads us around and around in safe, secure, unproductive circles.

Counting the cost and paying the price

One of the great old anthems of the faith is a hymn to the freedom of adventure: "Like a mighty army moves the church of God!/Brothers, we are treading where the saints have trod!" The church is not camped out for security, but moving forward against the gates of hell. We are in a war against spiritual darkness, and no war was ever won without paying a price.

My friend Jack knows what it means to live the adventure of faith. He also knows what it means to be afraid, and to pay a price. Jack is a missionary in one of the largest and most neglected mission fields in Christian history: the Muslim world. He is making Christian disciples in countries where evangelism is illegal, and where conversion to Christianity is punishable by imprisonment or death.

A few years ago, Jack and several of his associates were in a militant, fanatical Muslim country, preparing to begin a daring new penetration of that land with the gospel. Shortly after his arrival, Jack wrote a letter to his mother which concluded with these words: "I have peace, but also much fear." The day after he mailed that letter, Jack and his friends were arrested. They spent almost a year in prison for the crime of telling Muslim people about the love of Jesus Christ.

Jack was obedient to the call of God in his life, and he paid a price for that obedience. Undeterred, he is still reaching the Muslim world with the gospel. He continues to have peace in the knowledge he is doing God's will—and he continues to know fear.

Sometimes God delivers us from the furnace of our afflictions—and sometimes He gives us grace to stand the heat of that furnace. In Acts 7, the deacon Stephen didn't look for deliverance, but endured a martyr's death by stoning for the sake of Jesus Christ. Paul, in Philippians 3:10, didn't look for safety and security as he wrote, "I want to know Christ and the power of his resurrection and the fellowship of sharing in his sufferings, becoming like him in his death." Dietrich Bonhoeffer and Benigno Aquino did not look for deliverance or safety, but chose instead to follow their Lord and pay the heavy price of commitment.

Heaven is crowded with witnesses who can testify that while God does not promise to spare us from the trials of life, He is always *with* us in our trials, leading us through the fire. The healing choice for the hurt of fear is the decision to completely trust God with our lives, to risk everything for Him, and to truly live the adventure of the Christian life.

Not afraid to die

"In the real dark night of the soul," writes F. Scott Fitzgerald, "it is always three o'clock in the morning." The 3:00 A.M. fear that haunts the dark night of most human souls is the fear of death. This fear is common to mankind—though some of us try desperately to deny the reality of death. One poet has said, "Nothing can happen more beautiful than death." Another wrote, "Why fear death? It is the most beautiful adventure in life." There is something pitiable in these words—a poignant denial of the terrible truth of the grave.

There is nothing "beautiful" about death. First Corinthians 15:26 calls death an enemy to be destroyed, and Romans 5:12 says that death entered the world through sin, and now overshadows us all. So let's speak the truth: death is our enemy, a powerful destroyer. Many of the things we fear in life are so trivial or unlikely to occur that our worry is truly wasted—but death is truly worthy of our fears.

Fortunately, that's not all there is to know about this enemy called death. God has given us victory over the grave through the death and resurrection of Jesus Christ. Paul concludes 1 Corinthians 15 with these words of triumph: "Where, O Death, is your victory? Where, O Death, is your sting? . . . Thanks be to God! He gives us the victory through our Lord Jesus Christ." Though fully God, Jesus became a man in order to endure death, disarm it, and conquer its fear. Hebrews 2:14–15 tells us that Jesus took part in our humanity "so that by his death he might . . . free those who all their lives were held in slavery by their fear of death."

I am not afraid to die. I fear the physical suffering that may accompany my death. I have moments of anxiety when I contemplate the separation death will cause between myself and those I love. But I'm at peace with the reality of death because I'm convinced of the greater reality Christ has given us: "Because I live, you shall live also." I know I will live forever, not because of any good works I have done, but because by faith I have committed myself to Jesus Christ as my Savior and Lord. The healing choice for the fear of death is to commit ourselves to the resurrected Christ, to receive by faith the gift of eternal life He bought for us on the cross.

Several years ago, I and several others in my previous church in Minneapolis received a letter from a friend who was dying of leukemia. Only twenty-eight years old and approaching the close of her life, she wrote,

Many people have asked me if I feel any bitterness about my long illness and imminent death at a young age. No, I feel no bitterness or anger. Many people would demand to know, "Why me?" But I can't help but ask, "Why *not* me?"

I have felt so much pity for the millions of people starving to death all over the world, for those who are so poor they can barely subsist, for those who are physically handicapped. I can't expect that God owes me anything more than these people have—but God has given me more! My life has been filled with every blessing a person could want.

I was raised by loving parents, and I had a happy childhood. I've had eight years of marriage to a wonderful man. Our love has grown so much over the years that our marriage is much more beautiful now than when it began. I've been blessed by more precious friends than one could ever hope for.

My life has been permeated by a faith in the resurrected Christ. He has been my purpose in life. He has been my peace in death. So mourn for those that I leave behind, but don't mourn for me.

I'm not afraid to die because the resurrection of Jesus Christ is not just some doctrine to me; it's my *reality*. I've settled the matter of my own death, and that sets me free to truly live. The same can be true for you. I can think of no finer benediction to offer you than this: May you live your life courageously, victorious over your fears—and may you die gloriously in a great cause for Jesus Christ!

Epilogue

Joy—Even When It Hurts

We should be watchful lest we lose any blessing which suffering might bring.

—A. W. Tozer

In this you greatly rejoice, though now for a little while you may have had to suffer grief in all kinds of trials. These have come so that your faith—of greater worth than gold, which perishes even though refined by fire—may be proved genuine and may result in praise, glory and honor when Jesus Christ is revealed.

—1 Peter 1:6–7

The early years of Carolyn Koons's life were spent in a series of rough, dirty logging towns. Violence and mistreatment were just part of growing up for her. Her mother and father repeatedly abused her, and finally abandoned her on the streets.

As a teenager, Carolyn was befriended by some Christian young people who cared enough to patiently, persistently win this hardened young woman to Christ. Carolyn went on to college and seminary, eventually becoming a professor of Christian Education at Azusa Pacific University. In 1975, she founded Mexicali Outreach, an evangelistic ministry which takes hundreds of Christian students into northern Mexico for short-term missionary work. The first year she led a team to Mexicali, they toured a youth prison housing three hundred boys, some as young as five years old. There she met nine-year-old Tony.[1]

Tony was raised in the streets of Tijuana, surrounded by crime, narcotics, and prostitution. Tony's childhood, like Carolyn's, had been filled with violence and mistreatment. One day when five-year-old Tony was playing in the street, he heard his baby brother screaming. Tony went to the door of his house, heard a loud thud, and froze. The screaming had stopped. Looking inside, Tony saw his mother and father bending over his brother's body, a bloody club nearby.

Tony fled and his parents reported him to the police, accusing him of the murder. So five-year-old Tony was thrown into prison—and he stayed there for four years before being discovered by Carolyn Koons. There had never been any investigation of the charges against him.

After a long and expensive battle against bureaucratic red tape, Carolyn Koons won Tony's freedom and brought him to the United States, whereupon she found herself a single parent to a twelve-year-old boy. In the hardness and resentment of this terribly wounded boy, Carolyn confronted the scars of her own childhood. Her own long-buried hurts surfaced again as she sought to help Tony overcome his painful memories—and she *used* those hurts to bring healing into Tony's life. She saw the love of Christ begin to change his heart.

Today, Tony is a Christian college student at Azusa Pacific. Carolyn and Tony are living proof of the power of God not only to heal our hurts, but to *transform* our hurts into healing for others. Theirs is a story of the power of God to penetrate the darkness of human suffering with the light of *joy*.

Joy in our trials

The Bible promises that we can actually have *joy* no matter how hard our circumstances are. "Consider it all joy, my brethren, when you encounter various trials," says James 1:2 (NASB). Yet joy is usually the *last* thing we think of as we face our trials—and understandably so. The first thing that occurs to us in the hard places of life is not joy, but, "Why me? And why this? And why now?" When we're hurting, we have some questions to ask God—and God accepts our questions. He understands our hurt.

But there comes a time when we need to make the healing choice to move beyond our questions. We have to get on with our lives, even when it becomes clear that our hurts are not going to immediately go away. And the promise of God is that we can go on with *joy*.

How, then, do we find joy when we encounter various trials?

There is joy, first of all, in knowing that our trials have a purpose. James 1:3 says, "The testing of your faith develops perseverance." God is building endurance in us.

The Greek word for "testing" in this passage is *dokimos,* which means "approved." Many of the jugs and pots which have been unearthed in ancient ruins of Greece and the Middle East are marked on the bottom with this same word, *dokimos,* "approved." In this way, the valuable pieces of pottery were set apart. They had gone through the refiner's fire without cracking.

Similarly, when we go through the furnace of affliction and withstand the heat without cracking, then we build endurance, and we receive God's *dokimos,* His seal of approval. As Jesus described it in Matthew 25:23, this is the joy of hearing God say to us, "Well done, good and faithful servant! . . . Come and share your master's happiness!"

This is the kind of joy a man named Ignatius was learning to experience through a terrible trial of persecution. Ignatius was one of the early church fathers, the bishop of the church of Antioch in Syria. He was arrested by the Roman government for the crime of being a Christian, and sentenced to be executed for the Emperor's amusement in Rome. He was chained to a detachment of cruel, hardened Roman soldiers who led him on a forced march to Rome, a trek of over 1500 miles. Along the way, Ignatius wrote a letter to some Christian friends which included these words:

> The soldiers who guard me behave like animals, treating me with bewildering cruelty. They are like a pack of leopards, enjoying their sport, with myself as their prey. Still, this trial has its advantages. I'm growing accustomed to the ravages of leopards, which is just as well, since it will be real lions I face at Rome. As bitter as my present sufferings are, I am gaining spiritual endurance and mental fortitude for the trial that lies ahead.
>
> No power must hinder my going to Jesus Christ. Whether the path be fire or crucifixion or wild animals in the arena, I can bear it if it leads the way to Him, for He is my joy.

Ignatius willingly, courageously faced some of the cruelest trials imaginable—and he faced them with *joy,* knowing that he was building endurance, and that his trials led the way to Jesus.

A journey of discovery

I've sometimes observed two Christians suffering under similar trials, but making very dissimilar choices in their trials. One will choose to respond to his trial by giving up on life and wrapping himself in self-pity. The other will look for God's perspective on his hurts, and he will cooperate with God in *growing* through his trial. He prays for endurance, not mere escape—for joy, not mere comfort—and he always emerges from his trials a stronger and more joyful Christian.

Throughout our lives we are faced with tremendous opportunities. The problem is that these opportunities come disguised as unsolvable trials. Joy in the Christian life comes as we respond to our trials by allowing them to bring forth our character and wisdom and courage. These qualities reside in every human spirit; they are part of the image of God in which we are all molded. Whether these qualities are *displayed* in us in a time of crisis, however, depends primarily on the conscious choices we make: the choice to accept responsibility for our problems; the choice to take up the challenge of our trial rather than to moan about it; the choice to keep our gaze on God while glancing at our problems.

Life is a journey of discovery, and there is great *joy* in the adventure of spiritual and emotional growth. Sadly, most people just drift through life, evading its challenges, afraid of its risks. Unwilling to learn and to change, such people miss the deep joy of living. True joy is reserved for those who are willing to make the effort to *master* this thing called Life, to become *experts* in the art of growing with God and enjoying His grace.

If we are attentive, we can learn something new about the reality of God every day of our lives. Just think of all the ways, great and small, in which you've experienced God's goodness: a narrowly averted accident in your car or home; a letter or call from a distant friend; a new and unexpected insight into a passage of Scripture; a recovery from a painful illness; a sunny, fragrant, perfect day; a good friend or a good book that happened to come into your life at just the right time; that rare and inexpressible sense of well-being that sometimes comes upon us for no apparent reason.

The grace of God comes to us in many small ways that

we tend to overlook—or if we notice them at all, we ascribe them to "luck" or "chance" or "coincidence." But as we open our eyes widely to all the different ways God's grace is demonstrated in our lives, our day-to-day existence is dramatically transformed into a thrilling *adventure* of spiritual discovery. We gain a sense of direction and progress in our journey. No detail of life can be considered insignificant anymore, for now we see God's intimate involvement in every aspect of our lives. He is even involved with us in our hurts—and that heightened awareness of the presence of God brings us *joy*.

We all need some help along this journey to wholeness and joy. We need a few trusted Christian friends to whom we can disclose ourselves. God intended for us to be a *family* in the body of Christ—brothers and sisters who transparently share our hurts with one another. I really believe that only what we hide is going to hurt us.

Many of us have been brought up to believe it's a sign of weakness to confess our hurts and ask for help. Yet I'm convinced it's a sign of courage to admit we need help. Part of the job of mastering the art of living is *unlearning* what we have been taught about what it means to be mature. True maturity is proved not by stolid self-reliance, but by a willingness to be vulnerable and a desire to be known. The journey of spiritual discovery requires that we allow a few trusted people to see into the depths of our lives, so that we can mutually encourage each other toward maturity in Christ.

And some of us need to go a step further.

I've counseled many people over the years, and people often assume that a person who counsels others would have a handle on all his own problems. But the truth is that there have been times in my life when I have needed someone outside myself, listening to me and mirroring my feelings back to me, giving me a word of counsel to point me in the direction of wholeness.

There have been two occasions in my life when my hurts were so great that I knew I needed the help of a professional counselor. These two Christian psychologists were able to help me reassemble my broken self-image and to guide me further along the journey of spiritual discovery. As a result of the time I spent in counseling, I am today more whole and more effective as a Christian, as a husband, and as a father.

How about you? If you really want to be healed, then I

urge you to join me in doing whatever it takes to achieve that healing. Let go of your excuses and your pride, and open up your life to a few other Christian friends. If you are struggling with truly deep hurts, then begin now to seek the counseling you need.

You can begin by talking with your pastor, who can either help you or refer you to someone who is trained to help you with your particular problem. A friend who has been helped by counseling can also give you a reference. If finances are a problem for you, many churches have a counseling fund to assist people in getting help. Remember to seek a Christian counselor; many secular therapists see "religion" as the enemy of mental health and would not be understanding of your spiritual needs. Recognize, too, that people often become afraid of the effort and self-disclosure that's involved in becoming whole, and they drop out before any real progress has been made. When you begin counseling, make a commitment to persevere until you achieve genuine healing.

I invite you to join me in this quest for inner wholeness and maturity, and I wish you courage and endurance for your journey. But most of all, I wish you a deep and genuine sense of *joy,* even in your time of trial.

A glimpse of spring

Joe Bayly tells of an experience he had of joy in a time of trial, shortly after his five-year-old son died of leukemia. It was a windy, below-zero Saturday morning in January, and there was more than a foot of snow on the ground. Looking out the window of his home, Bayly saw the postal truck pull up to his mailbox. Without pausing to put on a coat, he ran out of the house, took the mail out of the box, and was about to rush back into the house when something among the letters caught his attention: a colorfully printed seed catalog.

On the front of the catalog were brilliant zinnias; on the back, luscious red tomatoes. Standing in his shirtsleeves, Bayly seemed not to even notice the cold as he leafed through the pages of roses, daffodils, dahlias, marigolds, corn, peas, and cucumbers. The fragrances of springtime seemed to rise from the pages, and for a brief moment the winter was past and he felt warmed and cheered.

Then the cold wind whipped up around him, and he rushed back inside and closed the door behind himself. Bayly later reflected on how our experiences as Christians are like that moment at the mailbox. "We feel the cold," he wrote, "just as those who do not share our hope, the biting wind that penetrates us as it penetrates them. But in our cold times, we have a seed catalog called The Bible. We open it, and we smell the promised spring, the eternal spring, and the first fruit that settles our hope is Jesus Christ, who was raised from death and cold earth to glory eternal." [2]

That is what our Christian joy is like—a fragrance of Christ and the coming spring amid the wintry trials of life. It's easy to give God praise when the sun is shining; it's another and much deeper thing to experience real joy when the bitter December wind is blowing hard in our faces and the light around us is failing.

Our lives are just a gleam of Time between two Eternities—but God is at work in our lives to fan that gleam into a shining glory, the glory of His own reflected image. The choice is ours: we can surrender to the cold and darkness of our trials—or we can allow God's light and warmth to shine through our lives in spite of our trials. In all the hurts you face in life, may you make the truly healing choice—the choice that leads to Christlike maturity, wholeness, and *joy.*

Notes

Chapter 1

1. John Gunther, *Death Be Not Proud* (New York: Modern Library, 1953).
2. Marie Rothenberg, *David* (Old Tappan, N.J.: Fleming H. Revell Co., 1985).
3. Ibid, 91.

Chapter 2

1. Paul Brand, "A Surgeon's View of Divine Healing," *Christianity Today,* 25 November 1983, pp. 15–16.
2. Kathryn Lindskoog, "What Do You Say to Job?" *Leadership* (Spring 1985):93–94.
3. M. Scott Peck, *The Road Less Traveled* (New York: Simon and Schuster, 1978), 239–40.
4. Charles Farr, *Leadership* (Spring 1985):16.
5. David Ireland, *Letters to an Unborn Child* (New York: Harper and Row, 1974), 117–18.
6. Kenneth L. Bakken, *The Call to Wholeness: Health As a Spiritual Journey* (New York: Crossroad Publishing, 1985), 11–12.
7. Norman Cousins, *The Healing Heart* (New York: Avon Books, 1984), 185–86.
8. Ron Lee Davis, *Gold in the Making* (Nashville: Thomas Nelson Publishers, 1983).
9. Lindskoog, "What Do You Say to Job?" 91.
10. Brand, "A Surgeon's View of Divine Healing," 20.

Chapter 3

1. John White, *The Golden Cow* (Downers Grove, Ill.: InterVarsity Press, 1979), 92–93.
2. C. S. Lewis, *A Grief Observed* (New York: Seabury Press, 1963), 11.
3. Ibid, 4.

4. Don Baker, *Pain's Hidden Purpose* (Portland: Multnomah Press, 1984), 63–64.

Chapter 4

1. Erich Fromm, *The Art of Loving* (New York: Harper and Row, 1956), 8–9.
2. Lloyd Ogilvie, *The Bush Is Still Burning* (Waco, Tex.: Word Books, 1980), 159.
3. *Newsweek,* 30 November 1981, p. 106.
4. Bruce Larson, *There's a Lot More to Health Than Not Being Sick* (Waco, Tex.: Word Books, 1981), 59.

Chapter 5

1. Peck, *The Road Less Traveled,* 32–33.
2. Lorraine Hansberry, *A Raisin in the Sun,* quoted in Tony Campolo, *It's Friday, but Sunday's Comin'* (Waco, Tex.: Word Books, 1984), 64–66.
3. Richard Selzer, *Mortal Lessons: Notes in the Art of Surgery* (New York: Simon and Schuster, 1976), 45–46.
4. Stephen D. Shores, *Discipleship Journal* 28 (1 July 1985):20.

Chapter 6

1. James Dobson, *Hide or Seek* (Old Tappan, N.J.: Fleming H. Revell Co., 1974).
2. *TV Guide,* 16 March 1985, pp. 5–10.

Chapter 7

1. A. W. Tozer, *The Root of the Righteous* (Harrisburg, Pa.: Christian Publications, 1955), 119.
2. T. M. Kitwood, *What Is Human?* (London: InterVarsity Press, 1970), 128.
3. Baker, *Pain's Hidden Purpose,* 34.
4. C. S. Lewis, *The Screwtape Letters.*
5. J. I. Packer, *God Has Spoken* (Downers Grove, Ill.: InterVarsity Press, 1979), 29.
6. C. S. Lewis, *Prince Caspian,* vol. 2 of *The Chronicles of Narnia* (New York: Macmillan, 1951), 135–36.

Chapter 8

1. David Augsburger, *Caring Enough to Confront* (Glendale, Calif.: Regal Books, 1980), 77–78.
2. A. W. Tozer, *Of God and Men* (Harrisburg, Pa.: Christian Publications, 1960), 75.

3. Josh McDowell, *Evidence That Demands a Verdict* (Arrowhead Springs, Calif.: Campus Crusade for Christ, 1972), 374.
4. Augsburger, *Caring Enough to Confront*, 53–54.

Chapter 9

1. Bob Considine, "Could You Have Loved This Much?" *Guideposts,* January 1966, pp. 4–7. Copyright 1966, 1985, by Guideposts Associates, Inc., Carmel, N.Y. 10512. Used by permission.

Chapter 10

1. Charles W. Colson, *Born Again* (New York: Bantam Books, 1976).
2. *Christianity Today,* 7 October 1983, pp. 53–54.
3. J. R. R. Tolkien, *The Hobbit.*

Epilogue

1. Carolyn Koons, *Tony: Our Journey Together* (New York: Harper and Row, 1984).
2. Joe Bayly, *The View from a Hearse* (Elgin, Ill.: David C. Cook Publisher, 1969), 120–21.

Acknowledgments

Robert Browning, in *Pauline* (1833), wrote to his dear friend Shelley, "Live forever, and be to *all* what you have been to *me.*" I would like to offer these words as a gift to all the special friends who have so significantly contributed to the development of this book.

My friend and brother in Christ, Jim Denney, has tirelessly edited, developed, and refined this book. His efforts are obvious on every page and every line, and there would have been no book without him.

Dr. Tom Granata, an outstanding Christian psychologist, has carefully critiqued each chapter of this book. His insights have contributed to both the biblical and psychological integrity of these pages. Tom has been my own personal friend and counselor for several years and has helped me gain greater understanding of my own trials. Many of the insights I share in this book were discovered through my relationship with Tom, and I will always be deeply grateful for his impact on my life.

For the past five years I have served as pastor of the First Presbyterian Church in Fresno, California, and many within our family of faith have contributed to the shaping of this book. My associate pastoral staff team of Dr. Ernest Bradley, Rev. Joe Pettit, Lydia Pugh, and Dr. Dwight Trowbridge have all added their loving suggestions and counsel to this book. I feel deeply privileged to be able to minister with such an outstanding staff.

Other friends from my church and my community who have offered suggestions, insights, and prayers during the writing of this book include Debbie Denney, Steven and Gayle Jaurena, Russ and Jan Koch, Jim and Carol Gartung, Hilary Chittick, Mike Flavin, Tess Mott, Meredith Hicks, Dr. Tom Griffin, Janet Nichols, Nancy Jen, Mary Lawrence Allen, Patricia Stivers, Bud Richter, Jim Helzer, Dr. Harold Haak, Lou Herwaldt, Bob Duncan, and Jeff Baggett. Many others in our congregation have also contributed to this work, and I am grateful for the friendship and insight of each one.

Dr. Bill Richardson, my life-long friend, offered his wise counsel to this material from the perspective of a Christian physician.

My new friend, Ernie Owen, Vice President and Editorial Director of Word Books, believed in the message of this book before it was ever committed to paper. I am very thankful for his suggestions, support, and encouragement.

I must acknowledge loving appreciation for my family. My wife, Shirley, and our children, Rachael and Nathan, have been a special support and encouragement to me throughout the months of study and preparation of the message in this book.

Finally, I am thankful to the scores of friends who have courageously permitted me to share the stories of their trials with you. Their transparency and vulnerability for the sake of others have given this book a dimension of realism and practicality that would otherwise have been impossible to achieve.